Precious
in His
Sight

Precious in His Sight

A GUIDE TO CHILD ADVOCACY

by
DIANA GARLAND
foreword by
MARIAN WRIGHT EDELMAN

New Hope
Birmingham, Alabama

Published by:
New Hope
P. O. Box 12065
Birmingham, AL 35202-2065

Scripture quotations identified NIV are taken from the *Holy Bible: New International Version* © 1978 by the International Bible Society. Used by permission of Zondervan Bible Publishers.

Scripture quotations identified RSV are taken from the Revised Standard Version, Old Testament section, © 1952; New Testament section, First Edition, © 1946, Division of Christian Education of the National Council of the Churches of Christ in the United States of America. Used by permission.

Dewey Decimal Classification: 361.7
Subject Headings: SOCIAL ACTION
                   ADVOCACY
                   CHURCH AND SOCIAL PROBLEMS
                   CHILD ABUSE

Cover illustration by Jeanie Holmgren

N927116•0493•5M1
ISBN 1-56309-081-3

About the Writer

Diana Garland, PhD, is the Dean of the Carver School of Social Work at the Southern Baptist Theological Seminary in Louisville, Kentucky. She is also the director of the Gheens Center for Christian Family Ministry and the organizer of the Southern Baptist Child Advocacy Network. She has authored, co-authored, or edited 11 other books, including *Christian Self-Esteem: Parenting by Grace, Covenant Marriage, The Church's Ministry with Families, Marriage for Better or For Worse,* and *Beyond Companionship: Christians in Marriage.* She and her husband, David, have two children, Sarah and John.

For Sarah and John
who taught me how precious children are.

Contents

FOREWORD

You hold in your hands a vital gift and tool, one that has the potential to help you and your church improve the lives of children and families in important new ways. Most of us have grown up in churches that teach and preach the precious value of children and the importance of service. Justice and compassion are familiar words, and ideals, to Christians. *Precious in His Sight*, however, offers an opportunity to look at children through new eyes: to behold their gifts afresh, to see their hurts, and to perceive new opportunities to serve children and families faithfully. And in looking at children with these new insights, we may glimpse the possibilities for redemption they offer to us, if we will only respond to what we see. How children are nurtured by their families, their churches, their communities, and their nation, has a profound impact that lasts a lifetime.

"He took a little child and had him stand among them. Taking him in his arms, he said to them, 'Whoever welcomes one of these little children in my name welcomes me; and whoever welcomes me does not welcome me but the one who sent me'" (Mark 9:36-37 NIV).

For many of us, when we think of our church's ministry to children, or how it "welcomes the child," the images that come to mind are of the children clustered around the minister for the children's sermon, or perhaps of the children in Sunday School. But what of the children whose physical, emotional, educational, and economic situations are depriving them of the opportunity to develop their God-given potential? Who is one such child we are called to welcome? We are called to welcome:

- one of the 2,400 children who is born into poverty each day;
- one of the 1,849 children who is abused or neglected each day;
- one of the 638 babies who is born to a mother who received late or no prenatal care each day;
- one of the 742 babies who is born too small to be healthy each day; and
- one of the 107 babies who dies each day before reaching his first birthday.

The religious community must renew and deepen its commitment to faithful child advocacy. The problems of child and family poverty, of discrimination, and of hunger and homelessness that confront this society are not problems that the religious community is required to solve alone. But they are problems on which Christians cannot turn their backs. Every person of faith has a special obligation to the poor and the powerless, and to seeking justice. As people of faith we can, and often do, make the case to others that investing in preventive programs and policies is "cost-effective." But the deepest and most enduring truth is that we must take better care of all of our nation's children because it is the right and moral thing to do. As ones who have been graced by Christ's compassion—His "suffering with"—and Christ's model of ministry that sought justice for the most vulnerable and marginalized, we too must minister with compassion and seek justice with and on behalf of the most vulnerable and marginalized children of our society, until each has the opportunity to develop to her or his God-given potential. It is that to which Christ calls us with the words, "Whoever welcomes one of these little children in my name welcomes me; and whoever welcomes me does not welcome me but the one who sent me" (Mark 9:37 NIV).

Committed individuals, organizations, and congregations can make life better for millions of children. The problems that too many of our nation's children see each day are very real, but they can be met if each one of us determines to make a difference in the lives of children. Together, we can see that no child is left behind.

We at the Children's Defense Fund seek, with your help, to create a new American paradigm in the 1990s that makes it un-American for children to grow up poor, unsafe, without basic health care, nutrition, housing, a strong early childhood foundation, or the education they need to develop to their God-given potential.

Please use *Precious in His Sight* to involve yourself and others in making that difference in your home, church, community, city, state, and nation. In Micah 6:8 we read, "And what does the Lord require of [us], but to do justice, and to love kindness, and to walk humbly with [our] God?"

Precious in His Sight will help you involve your congregation in study and in action. "Loving kindness," ministering through outreach in your community, is vital. However, much-needed private charity is a complement to, not a substitute for, public justice. Volunteers, however wonderful, cannot heal the millions of uninsured sick children, build the tens of thousands of housing units homeless young families need, or bolster the wages of millions of unemployed citizens. Use this book to learn how you can "do justice," extending your advocacy beyond the community to make your voice, and the voices of children, heard in the public policy and political process. Ask God for the wisdom to know what we faithfully and realistically can do. Then get righteously angry. Get inspired. Get involved. Demand action.

Our hope for children, ultimately, rests with God. It is God who gives us the faith and courage and strength to nurture and protect children. It is God who forgives us when we don't. Ask God for compassion to see the faces and hear the cries of children behind the statistics and stories.

I ask you to join with me and millions of people of faith on this journey of celebrating and loving our own, our congregations, and all of God's children, of taking on their joys and sorrows, of finding ways to help them grow and develop to their God-given potential, and of seeking justice for all of our nation's children. May God bless us on our journey. May we find joy and strength in one another as we join arm-in-arm with children.

In faith,

Marian Wright Edelman

ACKNOWLEDGMENTS

Several years ago, Marian Wright Edelman, president of the Children's Defense Fund, delivered a week of lectures on the campus of The Southern Baptist Theological Seminary. She spoke of the perilous condition of so many children and their families in our nation. She addressed our calling as Christians to care for children, and I was one of many whose heart was set afire. Since that time, I have been seeking ways that Southern Baptists might be a more effective voice for children; that we might find ways as individuals and as congregations to care for "the least of these."

As one step in that seeking, in 1990 and 1991, I called together a group of like-minded persons in various positions of leadership in Southern Baptist agencies and churches for a series of meetings at the Gheens Center for Family Ministry of The Southern Baptist Theological Seminary in Louisville, Kentucky. We explored ways to help Southern Baptists know and respond to the desperate needs of so many children in our society. We learned from one another about the work already going on to meet the needs of children and youth. I found myself amazed that so much was being done, but that we did not always know what was happening in our own denomination.

The group determined to continue the discussions so that we could work together more effectively. Thus, the Southern Baptist Child Advocacy Network was formed. We decided that a book was needed to highlight the needs of children, the teachings of the Bible concerning children, and concrete ways Christians and congregations can respond. The idea for *Precious in His Sight* was born, and I found myself with the exciting task of preparing this book. I am grateful for the encouragement of friends and colleagues of the Southern Baptist Child Advocacy Network. Robert Parham was especially helpful in the initial phases of planning this project.

Kathy Guy of the Children's Defense Fund has served as an invaluable consultant and supporter of this project and of the Southern Baptist Child Advocacy Network. Her *Welcome the Child*, a resource on child advocacy for churches, as well as the other excellent publications of The Children's Defense Fund, have been drawn from deeply in the preparation of *Precious in His Sight*. Shannon Daley and Gina Adams of CDF have also provided valuable support in the manuscript preparation.

I am grateful to The Southern Baptist Theological Seminary for providing me with sabbatical leave to work on this book. Dr. Robert Shippey, Associate Dean, has been an invaluable support in organizing the Southern Baptist Child Advocacy Network. My colleagues of the Carver School of Church Social Work at Southern have been an unfailing source of encouragement. Morling College, the Baptist College of New South Wales in Sydney, Australia, provided me with a haven for writing the manuscript.

Woman's Missionary Union, SBC, as represented by Karen Simons, believed in this project and encouraged me to pursue it to completion despite the inevitable obstacles along the way.

My family—David, Sarah, John, Dorsie, and Ned—have supported and helped me in this project, each in a special way. They have put up with me, believed I could do it, and encouraged me. I am grateful.

Although all these people contributed to this book, I alone am responsible for its errors and failings. I pray that God will use my effort, despite its limitations.

Diana Garland
July 4, 1992

1

Through Children's Eyes

"He took a little child and had him stand among them. Taking him in his arms, he said to them, 'Whoever welcomes one of these little children in my name welcomes me; and whoever welcomes me does not welcome me but the one who sent me'" (Mark 9:36-37 NIV).

Since Jesus spoke those words almost 2,000 years ago, the church has had the task of receiving children in Jesus' name. We teach children to sing, "Jesus loves the little children, all the children of the world. Red and yellow, black and white, they are precious in His sight. Jesus loves the little children of the world." [1] As Jesus set the example, so the church has tried to follow.

The early church was well known in Roman society for rescuing infants and children who otherwise would perish. If a Roman father did not lift up his new baby, who was ceremoniously placed at his feet, the child was exposed—left to die on the garbage heaps of the city. Christians sought out these infants and took them into their own homes. As the church gained a voice in society, it used that voice to attempt to stop the process of child abandonment. But the practice of child abandonment continued through the following centuries. In hard times, parents sometimes did not have enough food to feed all their children. The story of Hansel and Gretel is a story of attempted child abandonment. A stepmother, with her husband's consent, "lost" two young children in the forest because the family did not have enough food for both children and parents.

Child abandonment continued in Europe and America until the eighteenth century. In addition, many children were orphaned by wars and epidemics. In response, Christians continued to seek out and care for these children. They took children into their own homes and often adopted them. When the needs became too great, churches built institutions—orphanages and children's homes.

The abandonment of children in today's society is the consequence of our society's own kind of hard times—babies born to drug-addicted mothers; babies born with Acquired Immunodeficiency Syndrome (AIDS); children and teens who run away from home to escape abuse, or who are thrown out by their parents; and children of families overwhelmed by the numbing desperation of poverty. As Christians, we struggle to find ways to welcome these children, to receive them into our midst, and to care for them as Jesus taught us. This book looks at some of the ways Christians are caring for these children and their families, and ways you and your church can join in the caring.

We are concerned about children who are victims of social problems which seem as widespread and unstoppable as the practice of child abandonment in the Roman Empire. However, we are also concerned for our children—our sons and daughters, our friends' children, the children in our Sunday Schools and Vacation Bible Schools, the children in our communities. We are doing our best to care for and to love them. But there are sinister forces at work in our world which seem more powerful than our efforts to provide guidance and care, louder than messages we try to speak, more glitzy and attractive than the life-style we try to model. Today the world seems a much more frightening place to nurture children than did the world of our own childhood.

As we look back over our own childhoods, we survived much. Whatever generation we belong to, most of us grew up with our nation at war in faraway places. Those wars sapped our nation's strength, robbed some people of loved ones, and kept others in fear of such a loss. We lived with the threat of nuclear holocaust, with a helpless forboding that there was little we could do to protect ourselves or the ones we loved from total devastation. When today's young parents were children, they feared that nuclear war would come when they were away from home and their families.

We grew up watching the fabric of our society unravel. Patterns of living which seemed eternal gave way to the pressures of modern life. Economic recession and inflation drove many families into poverty, or to live on credit and depend on two incomes to survive. Changes in values concerning sex roles and the family made the family of "Father Knows Best" or "Leave It to Beaver"—the kind of family that, as children, we believed was "real"—look like a fairy tale. Few families today can afford the luxury of one parent working in the home as a full-time caregiver for the rest of the family. Many mothers, and some fathers, find themselves raising children without a partner to share the joys, the worries, and the responsibilities of parenting.

In fact, the declining birth rate and the lengthening life span have made families with dependent children in the home a minority group. Consequently, our adult-focused society gives little heed to the needs of children today.

THE WORLD OF CHILDREN TODAY

A World of Dilemmas

Children and youth in America today confront an array of challenges and difficulties. They differ in many respects from the challenges and difficulties we faced. These difficulties are the consequences of choices society has made and values embraced. Here are five of the difficult challenges which face, and sometimes overwhelm, today's children and youth.

1. Children are considered innocent and dependent, yet are put in situations that require them to act like adults long before they are ready. Children receive mixed messages. Society has not decided when a child is old enough to be left alone at home. For example, many school-age children spend hours alone at home each day while their parents are working. These parents would be considered neglectful if their children suffered harm while unsupervised. Consequently, school and community programs are helping children care for themselves when they are home alone, even though few really believe that they should be alone in the first place. Parents and children may be unhappy with this arrangement, but for many there seems to be no other option. Quality care for school-age children is nonexistent in many communities.

One community tried to develop an after-school activity program for children in the fourth, fifth, and sixth grades. Although many children wanted to participate, no one came. They couldn't! They had to stay home and take care of younger brothers and sisters. Not only were these 10- and 11-year-olds unsupervised, they were caring for even younger children. One research study found that children who spend long periods at home alone are more likely to be depressed, to drink alcohol, and to be sexually active (Jaffe, 1991, 25).

> David is ten years old. His brother, Shawn, is eight, and his sister, Missy, is six years old. David's father left while Missy was a baby. The family has not heard from him since. David's mother, Martha, dropped out of high school to get married at 18. She had never had a job. For the first year while Martha looked for work, the family survived on an Aid to Families with Dependent Children grant that provided them with less than $450 per month. Then Martha got a job as a nurse's aide, but her salary barely covered their rent and food. While Martha was working, a woman kept Missy and several other children in an apartment that had little space for children to play. The children often sat quietly and watched television. The woman did not charge much, however, and Martha did not make enough money to place Missy in a child-care center.
>
> For the past three years, David has been responsible for Shawn and Missy from the time school is out until his

mother comes home from work at 6:00. Before this year David would leave school and pick up Missy at the baby-sitter's apartment, so that his mother did not have to pay for an additional two and one-half hours of child care. This year Missy is in the first grade. When the children get home from school, David prepares an after-school snack. Then they watch television until their mother comes home. They are not allowed to play outside because Martha considers the neighborhood dangerous. Martha tries to call each afternoon to be sure that the children have arrived home safely.

Sometimes David would like to stay after school to play baseball with his friends on the school playground. He would also like to participate in the Boy Scout troop that meets weekly in the church next door to his school. He has not mentioned these things to his mother, however, because he knows she needs him to care for Shawn and Missy. He likes feeling responsible and has even begun to start supper for his mother some evenings. On the other hand, sometimes he wishes he could just be a kid.

Caring for themselves or being cared for is only one area in which children receive confusing messages. Children also receive confusing messages about sexuality. They are exposed to highly sexualized messages at every turn from the media, and in many communities, from peer groups. Parents often feel helpless when they try to challenge the dominant messages of our culture. For example, my husband and I try to screen the movies our children watch. But at a girls' sleep over party, our daughter, aged 11 at the time, watched *Pretty Woman*—a sexually explicit movie depicting values dissonant with Christian values concerning sexuality. The hostess's parents had rented the movie for the girls to watch. These parents also felt helpless and said, "It's not that much worse than television. If they don't watch it here, they'll see it somewhere else. They've seen it all, anyway."

Children have been exposed to sexuality for all of history. Long before the advent of television and movies, children slept in the same room with their parents, who were presumably sexually active. However, the difficulty with today's media is not just the exposure of children to sexual behavior, but the values about sexuality that the media promote. In movies and television, sexual relationships come first. Then, if two people like one another and are compatible, they consider becoming emotionally involved. Fear of AIDS has created some logistical problems, but the public message has been "be sure to use protection." Reconsidering the role of love and life-time commitment as the basis for sexual involvement is not promoted.

Consequently, it is hard to help children claim their place as children and to protect them from becoming involved in sexual relationships too early. Professionals tell children who have been sexually abused that they are not responsible for what has happened to them. The offender must bear total responsibility, even if the child has in some way encouraged sexual involvement. It is extremely difficult to convince some children that they are not at fault for what has happened to them. After all, they live in a world that encourages them to act on their developing sexuality and to be adults before they are ready. In this sense, society is sexually abusive of children.

2. Children are naturally curious and full of wonder; but adults are frightened by the complexity of the world that makes children so curious. Children have questioning minds that may lead in many directions. *How did the stars get up there, Daddy? How can God be everywhere? Why does God let children die in wars? Did Adam and Eve name the dinosaurs?* Children can learn that not all questions have easy solutions, and that adults do not know some answers.

Adults, however, are more frightened than children when they do not have answers. Because the knowledge base of our culture increases at such a rapid pace and issues become more complex, we want to plant our feet on solid ground. We want timeless answers we can count on. *God is in heaven, which is one right turn beyond the sun. God lets people die because He wants to take them home with Him. We are right and everyone else is wrong. If my answer doesn't fit what we now know about the world, then whoever was measuring the world must have measured wrong.*

Sometimes adults are afraid to tackle the complex knowledge of our age because their understanding of God does not allow room for growth. Adults may forget that God is bigger than their mental grasp. Consequently, children become confused and unwilling to trust adult answers that do not fit what they have experienced of the world and learned in school.

This is true of our understanding of relationships, too. We want relationships to be well-defined and simple. The 30-minute American television show says it all. There is much action and little dialogue—talking is usually short and to-the-point. Problems develop and are solved between the first and third commercial breaks, and we see everyone living happily ever after during the last 2-minute blip. We start living with the myth that family problems ought to be solved with a little dialogue, a lot of action, and once for all time. But life isn't like that for adults or children.

Children experience life differently from the way the media—and sometimes trusted adults— say it ought to be. Mom and Dad fight, but no one leaves. Maybe Dad even hits Mom, but everyone pretends it is not so. A big brother is involved in drugs, but a stern lecture from Mom does not seem to make any difference. Life crises don't always have happy endings. That has always been true. Today's adults are frightened by the complexities of the world, and they try to offer simple solutions for children and youth—solutions that are too simple for the world young people experience. Here is a glimpse of the world one young person faces.

Ben, aged 15, is confused and depressed. He has never been a good student. After drinking alcohol at a party six months ago, he became a steady drinker. His grades have dropped. His world fell apart a month ago, however, when his best friend, Carlos, was killed. Ben and Carlos had been on their way to play basketball in the park. They walked into an alley near their homes and unknowingly cornered a man in the act of raping a young girl from the neighborhood. Carlos tried to defend the victim and was stabbed.

Ben cannot understand why God allowed something like this to happen. Carlos was a Christian, an outstanding student, and well-liked by his friends. He had encouraged Ben to get his life straightened out, and it was because of Carlos that Ben was still in school at all. At the funeral, Carlos's pastor said that God had taken Carlos home to be with Him. He said that his friends and family should be joyful that God wanted Carlos with Him, out of the evil of this world.

Ben is far from satisfied. What kind of God would want Carlos when his family would be left with so much grief, and when his best friend would feel lost without him? What about the promise of Carlos's life? Ben feels guilty that Carlos is dead and not himself. It seems too much for Ben to figure out on his own, and certainly too big for him to do anything about.

3. Some children live in small, tight families. Others live in loosely-knit blended families made up of children and parents from former marriages. The average size of families is shrinking. Mobility causes families to be cut off from the extended family that helps with the tasks of growing up and parenting children. The average family size now is 1.8 children, and more and more children are "only" children. When "only" children marry one another, their children have no aunts, uncles, or cousins. Even in families with an aunt or uncle or two, there are still fewer family members to share the tasks and joys of child rearing than a generation ago. Many families live far from the relatives they do have. Telephones help us to "reach out and touch" one another with a phone conversation, but relatives who live halfway across the country cannot provide an evening's child care. Faraway relatives cannot provide the Sunday afternoon outings which make a child feel special to someone other than parents.

Other children are growing up in a radically different kind of family created by divorce and remarriage, the "blended family." Blended families consist of a married couple with one or more children from previous marriages. Some children are in the blended family only part of the time and live with their other biological parent the rest of the time. They may have four or more sets of grandparents and step-grandparents, aunts and uncles, and cousins to relate to in varying degrees of closeness.

Divorce and remarriage are hard for children, though living with parents who are constantly battling is also difficult. Children suffer when a parent leaves, especially when the leaving parent does not work hard to maintain a consistent relationship with the child. Often the remarriage of parents is a greater crisis for children than the divorce itself. Children have to shift into a different family system and many children do not feel anchored anywhere.

Kathy's parents recently divorced after three years of conflict and short separations. Kathy is five years old, and all that she remembers of her parents' marriage is fighting and unhappiness. As part of their divorce agreement, her parents decided to share custody and time with Kathy. Kathy spends alternate weeks with each parent. She has a different set of clothes, toys, neighborhood friends, and churches in each of her two homes. Consequently, she is never at home.

The situation became even more difficult for her when both parents remarried. Kathy went from being the sun around which her parents' lives revolved to a much less significant member of two families. In one home, Kathy's new stepfather has three children ages two, six, and seven. The six-year-old girl, Heather, moves into Kathy's room on weekends when she visits her father. Kathy feels moved aside in her mother's household. In her other home, Kathy's new stepmother has full custody of her three-year-old son, so that he is always with Kathy's father and stepmother. Kathy feels replaced by her cute stepbrother for the affection of her father in his household.

4. Children face a world of technologies which require more education to operate and which dominate the education and values of people. The development of values, however, has not kept pace with the development of technology. For example, look at the marvels of medicine that can help a two-pound premature infant survive, or allow doctors to successfully perform surgery on an unborn fetus. In dramatic contrast, our country has an abysmal record of preventive health care for children. More American children die from poverty in a five-year period than the total number of American battle deaths during the Vietnam War (Edelman, 1987, 29). We are tied with South Africa for last place among 20 industrialized nations in preventing infant death in the first year of life. Singapore, Hong Kong, Spain, and Ireland do better in preventing the deaths of babies. Babies of mothers who do not receive prenatal care are three times more likely to die in their first year of life (Edelman, 1987, 53). Yet in the United States, one out of four babies is born to a mother who receives no prenatal care (Children's Defense Fund, 1991, 62).

The Persian Gulf War showed the stark contrast between our attention to technology and our attention to the needs of children. Children and adults were fascinated by the videotapes of "smart bombs" seeking out and destroying their targets. My nine-year-old son said, "Mom, why can we build "smart bombs" but we can't build homes for homeless families?" Perhaps part of the answer lies in our attraction to the precision of technology, rather than to chronic human problems that cannot be solved by moving a joy stick.

In contrast to our fascination with war technology in the winter of 1990, was the horror of learning that infants were being left with grandparents or neighbors because both parents serving in the military were sent overseas. Our technology astounded the world, but our inattention to the needs of children and families came to light. We had planned with great precision and at great cost how to destroy the enemy, but had given no attention to the needs of our nation's children. A reservist who was called to duty pled for enough time to wean her baby before going overseas. The evening news featured a young couple writing to their eight-month-old baby left at home with a grandparent.

The cry went up, *How could parents be so unthinking as to both sign up in the military when they have children?* Many parents struggle to balance the demands of careers and the needs of their children. That was not new to us. That struggle is considered a private issue, one that parents are expected to manage. This time, however, the struggle became public because the employer was the American people. The issue was not just the possibility of neglect, but the possibility of leaving children orphaned. Most of us blamed the parents. Our outrage came in part because we were preparing for the eventualities of war in faraway places, but not addressing the reality of parents who felt they could best support their families by enlisting in the armed services. The private decisions of parents caused us to look at whether they should bear all the responsibility and cost of decisions about their children's needs. Perhaps their children are our children, and we should try to say something about their future, especially when their future is at risk. As parents decide to join the armed services, should we examine the effects of those decisions on their children? Should we also examine the overwhelming responsibility we ask of all parents to make right decisions about their children's future, with little support and guidance from others?

5. Some children have it all; other children live in poverty. Both suffer. Society has commercialized children with expensive brand name sports shoes and designer jackets to the extent that frustrated have-not teens have shot and killed other teens in order to steal their shoes. Some parents have tried to instill different values. They bought less expensive but functional clothing for their children, only to learn that their children were ridiculed and teased by their peers. Parents cringe at the thought that their children might be ridiculed. All of us, both adults and children, feel like hostages to the commercialism of our culture.

Middle class children must not only have certain things to be "in," but they must also participate in certain activities. Parents believe this too, sometimes even more than the children. Parents want to be sure that their children do not miss anything. We want to nurture our children's growth and development. Consequently, some children rarely play back and forth across the neighborhood lawns in the hours after school. Instead, they are in an endless procession of practice sessions for ballet, sports leagues, cotillion, scouts, and church activities. One overseas visitor commented that it seems that American children are being raised in moving vehicles (Bronfenbrenner, 1990, 35). There seems to be little time for creative play, for "wasting" an afternoon reading a book, or seeing how big a tower you can build out of crackers and peanut butter. Instead, children are constantly performing or practicing to perform. Then they can show the world that their parents are good parents who develop their children's gifts and abilities. These children live in a pressure cooker of expectations.

In contrast, the world many children face is as barren and chaotic as the world of middle-class children is enriched and structured. They live in poverty. Children are the poorest population group in our country, and they are getting poorer. A total of 12.6

million American children now live in poverty, an increase of more than 2.5 million in only ten years (CDF, 1991, 23). One out of five children lives in a family below the poverty level. Their parents must choose between feeding their children, paying the rent or utility bills, or taking their children to the doctor.

Welfare (Aid to Families with Dependent Children) only reaches about half of poor children. Welfare provides less than four dollars per day to support a child. Food Stamps provide 50 cents per meal (CDF, 1991). There is no extra money for brand name sports shoes or soccer league fees. Yet these children are exposed to the same commercialization as middle-class children. Often they respond with anger or hopelessness.

A ten year old, whom we will call Anthony, described what it is like to live in a poor, single-parent family:

> Sometimes it's sad because I feel different from other kids. When other kids get to go to fun places, I can't. I don't have enough money and they do.
>
> Most of my friends get an allowance, but I don't because my mom doesn't have enough money. They get to buy things they want and need, and I don't. The other day in school we had this balloon contest, and it only cost one dollar. Out of three years I haven't been able to get one.
>
> Me and my brother are a little hard on shoes. This summer the only shoes we had were thongs. When church time came, the only shoes we had to wear were one pair of church shoes. The one that got them first got to wear them. The one that didn't had to wear a pair of my mom's tennis shoes or my sister's.
>
> I have a big brother. He is not my real brother. He is with the Big Brothers and Big Sisters Association (a volunteer organization). Once I tried to tell my big brother about welfare. It was so embarrassing I was about to cry. I don't like Joe just because he takes me to a fun place

every week; I like Joe because he makes me feel special.
Sometimes I pray that I won't be poor no more and
sometimes I sit up at night and cry. But it doesn't change
anything. Crying just helps the hurt and the pain. It
doesn't change anything.
One day, I asked my mom why the kids always tease
me. She said it's because they don't understand. But I do
understand about being on welfare and being poor, and it
can hurt (Guy, 1991, 28).

Not only are many children poor, but many have no home.
Today there are 100,000 homeless American children; nearly one
of four homeless people is a child, and the numbers are growing
each day.

Darlene was born when her mother was only 16.
Darlene was raised by her mother and grandmother in a
small apartment in the slums of one of our nation's poorest cities. Darlene was determined to get out of poverty.
Darlene had a reading disability, however, and with little
encouragement at home, she fell further and further
behind in school. When she was 16, her boyfriend, John,
aged 18, encouraged her to come with him to a western
city where John's brother promised to help them find jobs.
Darlene saw this as her chance and went with John.
They discovered that there were no good jobs for high
school dropouts. Darlene and John both took jobs in fast-
food restaurants at minimum wage. Soon Darlene learned
she was pregnant, and Robert was born six weeks prema-
turely, ten months after Darlene left home. With his
dreams frustrated and growing demands that he could not
seem to meet, John became abusive. After a violent argu-
ment, Darlene made John leave. She was still working at
the fast-food restaurant.

Brenda, another single teenaged mother who lived in the same building, kept Robert while Darlene worked. Darlene was able to pay some of her bills for a couple of months, but she fell further and further behind. She had never had to manage money before, and there was so little to manage. When Robert was almost two years old, she found herself evicted from her apartment because she had not paid the rent. For the next six months, she lived with different friends, trying to help some with their living expenses. Her baby-sitter became frustrated with Darlene's inability to pay regularly, and refused to keep Robert. Consequently, Darlene lost her job because of excessive absences from work. Her friends were no longer willing for her to stay with them, especially since she had no money to contribute toward groceries or rent. The weather was too cold to sleep outside, so she and Robert moved into a shelter for homeless families.

In fact, Darlene and her son are a pair of homeless children, one trying to parent the other. Darlene is discouraged and feels hopeless; she has little emotional energy for loving and encouraging the development of an active two-year-old. She cannot provide Robert with the secure, stable environment he needs to develop emotionally and intellectually. Homelessness has a devastating effect on children; half of homeless preschoolers are developmentally delayed and/or clinically depressed (Dail, 293).

Today's children live in a world of stark contrasts:
- between being dependent children and being on their own with adult responsibilities and decisions;
- between simple answers and a complex, mystifying world that is sometimes beyond understanding;
- between families so small the few adults cannot wrap themselves around all the demands on them and families so loose

that children have little sense of security and belonging; and
- between having it all and being pressured to do it all, and having nothing and feeling hopeless that tomorrow will be any different.

The "Normal" Crises of Childhood

On this canvas of societal crises, we paint the crises that children face just because they are children: worrying about what will happen to them if Mommy and Daddy get sick or die; being teased or rejected by other children at school; doing poorly in math or English. All children struggle as adolescents between the dependence on parents that signifies childhood and the self-reliance that characterizes adulthood. They contend with the pressures of the peer group to do things they know are wrong. Small children have to learn that when they are left in the church nursery, Mom or Dad will come back. Adolescents have to cope with their developing sexuality. Children must learn to cope with teachers who aren't fair, with bullies on the playground, and with fears of monsters— both the ones under the bed and the ones who wear Arab clothing and might force parents to leave them and go to a faraway war.

As adults, we wonder how our children will find their way through all of these personal and social issues to become responsible, faithful, courageous, creative adults. As much as we try to be prepared to respond to our children's needs, to be sensitive to the distress signals children give, we know that it is not enough. We feel small in the face of the challenges. We wonder who will fight poverty, commercialization, and family crises that make the way to adulthood for many children an even more hazardous journey.

We worry about our own children. We wonder what will happen to the children of others, the children hidden away in ghettos and in rural poverty. The early church responded to the overwhelming needs of children by taking them in. They challenged a culture which said that unwanted children had no value. We too, are called to respond.

"WHOEVER RECEIVES ONE SUCH CHILD
IN MY NAME RECEIVES ME"

Jesus taught us to seek out children. Wondering and worrying about the welfare of children beyond our own circles of concern are not enough. Jesus opened the circle of concern, welcomed children, and made a place for them when the disciples wanted to shut them out.

"People were bringing little children to Jesus to have him touch them, but the disciples rebuked them. When Jesus saw this, he was indignant. He said to them, 'Let the little children come to me, and do not hinder them, for the kingdom of God belongs to such as these.' And he took the children in his arms, put his hands on them and blessed them" (Mark 10:13-14, 16 NIV).

Taking time to be with children made a dramatic statement in Jesus' day. For a scholar to spend time with children except in formal teaching was considered a waste of time (Weber, 1979). But Jesus did more than simply make time for children; He turned the world's values upside down and placed children first.

"At that time the disciples came to Jesus and asked, 'Who is the greatest in the kingdom of heaven?' He called a little child and had him stand among them. And he said: 'I tell you the truth, unless you change and become like little children, you will never enter the kingdom of heaven. Therefore whoever humbles himself like this child is the greatest in the kingdom of heaven" (Matt. 18:1-4 NIV; see also Mark 9:34-35).

In the kingdom of God, the smallest is the greatest. The kingdom belongs to children. Jesus told His listeners, "Anyone who will not receive the kingdom of God like a little child will never enter it" (Luke 18:17 NIV). Children are our example. Moreover, Jesus taught that "if anyone causes one of these little ones who believe in me to sin, it would be better for him to have a large millstone hung around his neck and to be drowned in the depths of the sea" (Matt. 18:6 NIV). At the end of time, God will count our care for the hungry, the thirsty, the stranger, the naked, the sick, and the imprisoned as our care of Christ Himself (Matt. 25:34-40). Caring for children is caring for Jesus; it expresses our love and welcome of God with us.

> "He took a little child and had him stand among them. Taking him in his arms, he said to them, 'Whoever welcomes one of these little children in my name welcomes me; and whoever welcomes me does not welcome me but the one who sent me'" (Mark 9:36-37 NIV).

Jesus was not simply using a child as a symbol or metaphor. He was commending actual children to our care.

Scriptures clearly point to God's concern and presence with the poor, the oppressed, the orphaned. The orphans in our own culture are not only those orphans who have no biological parents, but those who have been socially orphaned, left without an inheritance of hope, resources, and opportunities for the future. Our orphans are today's throwaway children—the homeless, the school dropouts, the chemically dependent, the poor, the abused, and the troubled. God listens to their plight.

> "You hear, O Lord, the desire of the afflicted; you encourage them, and you listen to their cry, defending the fatherless and the oppressed, in order that man, who is of the earth, may terrify no more" (Psalm 10:17-18 NIV).

"A father to the fatherless, a defender of widows, is God in his holy dwelling. God sets the lonely in families" (Psalm 68:5-6a NIV).

Repeatedly, the Old Testament prophets called for the people of God to work for justice:

"Do not take advantage of an orphan. If you do and they cry out to me, I will certainly hear their cry"(Ex.22:22-23).

"Speak up for those who cannot speak for themselves, for the rights of all who are destitute. Speak up and judge fairly; defend the rights of the poor and needy" (Prov. 31:8-9).

"Is not this the kind of fasting I have chosen: to loose the chains of injustice and untie the cords of the yoke, to set the oppressed free and break every yoke? Is it not to share your food with the hungry and to provide the poor wanderer with shelter—when you see the naked, to clothe him, and not to turn away from your own flesh and blood? Then your light will break forth like the dawn, and your healing will quickly appear; then your righteousness will go before you, and the glory of the Lord will be your rear guard. Then you will call, and the Lord will answer; you will cry for help, and he will say: Here am I. If you do away with the yoke of oppression, with the pointing finger and malicious talk, and if you spend yourselves on behalf of the hungry and satisfy the needs of the oppressed, then your light will rise in the darkness, and your night will become like the noonday. The Lord will guide you always" (Isa. 58:6-11a NIV).

As Christians, we need to work to loose the chains of poverty that create discouragement and despair. We need to untie the bonds of commercialization that distort children's values. We need to set children free to become all that the Father has created them to be. We need to strengthen small families and large blended families. We need to strengthen middle-class families and families living in the desperation and hopelessness of poverty. We want to be sure that every child lives in a family that can decently and with dignity provide for basic needs of shelter, clothing, food, and hope for the future.

"WHAT IS GOOD, AND WHAT THE LORD REQUIRES OF US"

Too often we read stories like those of David, Kathy, Ben, Anthony, and Darlene and her son, and we feel overwhelmed. We seem to have such small voices, such limited resources in the face of the problems which confront children and families. Caring without action, however, is empty. God will not be concerned on the last day with whether we worried about the hungry or the shelterless. God will be concerned with what we did about their needs. Welcoming all our children takes great personal courage and faith in a God who can take a few loaves and fish and do great things with them. The expectations God has for us are very clear:

> "He has showed you . . . what is good; and what does the
> Lord require of you but to do justice, and to love kindness,
> and to walk humbly with your God?" (Mic. 6:8 RSV).

To do justice
God requires us "to do justice"—to speak out in behalf of those with no voice. It is easy to love our own children, to care for those children in our midst. It is harder to look beyond the lovable children that touch us, to the systems that hurt children. It is hard to

figure out the complex issues that insidiously destroy families. But over and over, the Bible calls us to do justice, to minister not only to the needs of persons who have been hurt by society's injustice, but to speak out against the injustice itself.

And to love kindness

Justice concerning the issues which face children needs to be rooted in a love of kindness. Kindness requires a face-to-face relationship with another. **Kind**-ness connotes relating to others as our own kind, our kindred. We are to relate to others as our own families. It is not enough to care for all children in general; we also need to care for specific children as our own. Jesus taught us to receive children into our midst, to bless them and touch them, to make them a part of our lives. Their thoughts, feelings, and needs have meaning for us, and our doing justice has a life to it that comes from firsthand caring for children.

Relating to and caring for children demands that we know them. Children are not smaller versions of adults. They see the world through different eyes. They have different ways of thinking about and understanding the world. Loving kindness means learning how and taking time to relate to children.

- You are *loving kindness* when you listen to a child and know how the world looks to her. To sit down and talk with a child, giving her all your attention and not just a pat on the head or a quick question about school—that is loving kindness.
- You are *loving kindness* when you read about children's development as spiritual, emotional, and social beings. To care enough to take time to learn what the world is like from a child's perspective—that is loving kindness.
- You are *loving kindness* when you find ways to make friends with children, especially children who need a friendly adult in their lives. To seek out an Anthony who needs a friend to help him cope with the injustices of life—that is loving kindness.
- You are *loving kindness* when you allow a child to lead you in

worship and ministry. To make way in your church for children to light a candle, read a prayer or a Scripture, play the worship prelude, or go with you to visit the sick—that is loving kindness.

• You are *loving kindness* when you recognize that the most important lover of a child is that child's parent and when you find ways to empower that parent to love. When you are a friend to a lonely, isolated parent and you help that parent to have hope for the future and skills for loving and living with his or her child—that is loving kindness.

And to walk humbly with your God

The dragons we want to slay in behalf of our children may seem too strong and powerful for us—poverty, homelessness, educational failure, commercialization, glamorization of sexual promiscuity. We may feel that we only have a widow's mite, stones and a slingshot, and a few loaves and fishes. Unless we abide in the love and promises of our Saviour, we can do nothing with such feeble resources. But we have been promised that if we abide in Christ, if we keep our hand in His, our work will be fruitful; "ask whatever you wish, and it will be given you" (John 15:1-7). Whatever else we do, our doing justice and our loving kindness must be the fruit of our walk with God, and must be accompanied by our prayers for God's leadership and presence in our doing and loving.

> "Do not be anxious about anything, but in everything, by prayer and petition, with thanksgiving, present your requests to God. And the peace of God, which transcends all understanding, will guard your hearts and your minds in Christ Jesus. Finally, brothers, whatever is true, whatever is noble, whatever is right, whatever is pure, whatever is lovely, whatever is admirable—if anything is excellent or praiseworthy— think about such things. I can do everything through him who gives me strength" (Phil. 4:6-8, 13 NIV).

WHERE FROM HERE?

We are to be advocates for children. In this book, the word *children* refers to youngsters from infancy through the teen years—they are our children. I will focus on children growing up in the United States, recognizing that children around the world also need our voices to speak in their behalf. An advocate is one who stands up and speaks out for others. An advocate confronts injustice and supports just ways in which people can live together. Here are some examples of child advocacy.

•You are afraid of what might happen if your youngster visits the homes of friends while their parents are not home; they may experiment with drugs or alcohol or engage in other dangerous or inappropriate activities. You just learned that such a party took place, involving your child and several others. If you call other parents and meet together informally to talk about some basic rules, such as calling one another to be sure that a parent is present before approving attendance at parties or overnight visits, you are a child advocate.

•You are concerned that children are not included in the worship of your church. If you go to the worship committee to discuss the involvement of children in worship leadership and to ask them to consider reorganizing the worship service in ways that will engage children, you are a child advocate.

•You are concerned about children like David in your community, children at home alone each day after school. If you talk with your church about finding ways to offer an after-school program for children of poor working parents, you are a child advocate.

•You are worried about undereducated teen parents with bleak prospects and few resources for giving their own children hopeful futures. If you write to your congressional representatives asking them to vote for a bill that makes more money available for day care for low-income children and for educational programs for young parents, you are a child advocate.

Some people believe that child advocacy threatens parents, adults, and teachers. Child advocacy, however, does not try to take power away from adults; instead, it seeks ways to empower parents, teachers, and other adults with the resources they need to shape nurturing environments for children. This book is about children and families our nation is failing, families who need Christians to advocate for justice.

The rest of this book explores ways you and your church can care for "the least of these" through ministry with specific children and their families. It suggests ways to become advocates of justice for children, especially those with the greatest needs. I have suggested community people with whom you might talk and activities to help you discover children's needs in your community. These suggestions are based on the assumption that you will be studying these issues in your church's missions organization, a mission action group or committee, or in another church group setting. Of course, you may also want to read the book on your own. However, Jesus sent people out in ministry by twos, and I hope you will involve others in your congregation in your concern and action for children. You will be strengthened, and others will have the opportunity for spiritual growth through ministry.

Chapter 2 explores the place of children in our churches. In chapters 3 through 6, we will look at some of the dragons which threaten children today. The specific issues addressed are inadequate and substandard child care, poverty and homelessness, school failure, teen pregnancy, substance abuse, child abuse, and family crises. In chapter 7, we will look at doing justice as Christians, and how to speak out in support of public policies and structures that care more effectively for children and their families.

[1] Words: "Jesus Loves The Little Children" alt. by C. H. Woolston. Word alt. © 1991 Broadman Press (SESAC). All rights reserved. Used by permission.

2

Welcoming Children

Churches take seriously the responsibility of caring for children. Many church programs focus specifically on the needs of children. Sunday School classes, missions organizations, and recreational programs engage children and youth in learning the Christian faith and the Bible. Children and teenagers experience the caring of their community of faith through the nurture and concern of faithful adult leaders. Many churches also provide worship services specifically for preschoolers and children, so that they do not have to sit quietly through an adult meeting that does not interest them.

However, children also need to be included in meaningful ways in a community of people of all ages. Children need to be included with adults in the life of the faith community because life in our larger society has become so age segregated. Children spend their days in groups of peers in school or child care. Parents work in offices away from their children. The friendships of adults and children are often formed in these age segregated settings, so that friendships are developed person-to-person rather than family-to-family. Consequently, children have few close relationships with adults other than parents and teachers. Social occasions no longer include family and friends of all ages. Instead, children invite their peers, and adults invite other adults. Children are left in the care of a baby-sitter or a video cassette player in another room.

Too often, churches become mirrors reflecting this age segregation of our society. In many congregations, adults seldom see children, except to move out of the way when they run down the church hallways at the end of a morning or evening of activities. Adults do not have opportunities to know children, unless they lead one of the children's activities. Children do not have opportunities to know adults, except those who lead them. Children have few adults who relate to them just because they want to. Adults tend to relate only to groups of children for whom they are responsible. It is difficult for adults to be sensitive to the needs of children if they do not know any children personally. Children need advocates who will speak in their behalf in the church community, because they seldom are able to speak for themselves. It is hard to care for people—children—we do not know; it is easier to remain blind to their needs, their concerns, and their gifts.

Adults and children learn about the family of God by being members of it. Adults and children including preschoolers need to participate in community life with one another, benefit from one another's gifts, and care for one another's needs. Teaching needs to be accompanied by meaningful experiences in which adults and children can participate together and know one another. A community of faith is an extended family of babies, crawlers, toddlers, runners, and those with walkers and wheel chairs worshipping together—pilgrims journeying together in a covenant community.

Children learn best from experiences. They learn about God's love by being loved by God's people, about being a child of God by belonging in God's family of faith, about worship by worshipping with all God's people, about ministry by serving the needs of others alongside adults. Adults, too, learn by experience. They learn to value the contribution children can make to their lives by experiencing that contribution. They learn to understand the world from a child's eyes by listening to a child. By relating to children, adults can learn to "become like a little child."

Requiring small children to sit next to their parents through a long worship service they cannot understand does not include them much more than sending them to a separate worship service. Children and youth need to be actively included as valued participants and leaders in worship, Christian care, administration, and ministry in a church community.

WELCOMING CHILDREN IN OUR MIDST

Worship

Providing children with worship services separate from parents has not been entirely for the benefit of children. Separate children's worship allows parents and other adults to worship without being disturbed by whispering, wiggling, bored children who ask to go to the rest room and drop hymnbooks during silent prayer. Children interrupt worship just like they interrupt quiet meals and restful sleep. If we want children to discover the God of grace and learn to participate in the community of faith, we will have to accept the interruptions which come with including children (Aleshire, 1988, 95). We have to look for ways to involve children in worship, rather than expecting them to sit quietly while parents worship.

A beginning step toward balancing the age segregation of church programs with age integration is to organize a special day for including and recognizing children as members of the community. Many churches celebrate a Children's Sabbath and/or Youth Sunday, when children or youth have primary roles in the worship. Denominational publications provide sermon outlines, suggested hymns, responsive readings, and prayers that recognize and celebrate children. Such special services can highlight a particular need of children, such as quality child care for low-income families. These services may include the congregation in some advocacy effort, such as providing stationery and addresses in the worship bulletin to encourage members to write to legislators about a specific issue as part of an "offering of letters." A worship emphasis may also include attention to the ministries of the church through denominational agencies that care for children and their families in crisis. Care needs to be taken that such worship services genuinely include the children in ways they understand, so that the service calls the whole church—adults and children—into worship, prayer, and ministry. In other words, the focus of the service is not simply *about* children; it also *includes* them.

Some churches make deliberate efforts to include children in the ongoing life of the congregation. Some Sunday School classes provide cross-generational programs so that people of all ages can participate in Christian education together. In worship, children light candles, collect the offering, read Scripture, and gather on the steps of the pulpit for the children's sermon. Bulletins for children explain the different worship activities, provide an outline of the sermon, ask questions which children can answer by listening, and provide puzzles and games related to the worship theme. These worship aids give children an activity to do which relates to what they hear. Music can be sung by all, sometimes with clapping hands. People are called into and included in worship in a wide variety of ways. Music, prayers, reading together, symbols, and colors all add to the richness of worship and invite people of all ages to communion with God and with one another.

Unfortunately, we too often confuse worship with a performance which the congregation quietly watches and listens to. But worship should actively include the whole congregation. Lay leaders of different ages encourage participation. Ways children and youth can participate as worship leaders include:

- reading prayers or responsive readings they have written;
- reading missionary correspondence to the congregation during the weekday prayer service;
- writing new words to traditional hymn melodies and teaching them to the congregation (Heusser, 1985, 40);
- creating signs, banners, or arranging flowers and other objects from God's creation on a table in the sanctuary;
- playing a special part in the music—clapping hands, ringing small bells which are then collected in an offering plate so as not to tempt children to accompany the sermon;
- using sign language as they sing;
- playing instruments (violin, recorder, etc.) for which they are taking lessons along with piano and organ during hymns or

during the prelude or postlude;
- leading a responsive reading, either as an individual or as one of a group of children or youth;
- singing in a children's or youth choir or a family choir composed of persons of all ages;
- performing in a brief skit related to the Scripture reading;
- greeting persons at the door, particularly other children and youth who may be visiting, and asking to sit with them during the worship;
- collecting the offering.

Some ways to encourage children to feel included as worship participants:
- provide special bulletins or bulletin inserts with children's activities related to the worship theme;
- pray for things that children and youth are thankful for or concerned about;
- ask children before worship what they want the congregation to pray for, and include their concerns along with others of the congregation;
- provide at least a portion of the sanctuary with a carpeted floor where small children's feet and movement will make less noise and where children can sit and work quietly with crayons and paper;
- encourage young children to sit with their parents who are in the choir;
- include imagery, stories, and applications during the sermon that relate to children's and teens' experiences;
- divide the sermon into two or more sections of about ten minutes, interspersed with singing and responsive readings (Armstrong, 1988).

Ways used to encourage children and youth to participate in worship also encourage greater participation and deeper worship among adults as well. Worship is more than an intellectual exercise. Many of us find that we remember the children's sermon and the prayerful singing of a praise chorus longer than the more sophisticated adult sermon which follows. Adults, too, benefit from being encouraged to make concrete applications of the principles of our faith, from being included actively in the worship experience, and from experiencing variety in the worship hour that keeps their attention. Rather than having separate messages for children and adults, while the other group "eavesdrops," all are considered part of the same group of believers.

At other times, it is appropriate and helpful for children to be separated from adults, just as parents and children in a family need time apart as well as together. Each congregation must find its own balance, built around the needs of both children and adults.

Christian Care

Some churches include children and youth in the Christian care of visiting the ill and the homebound. An adult and child serve together as a Christian care team. Just as adults need help in learning to provide Christian care to persons in the crisis of illness or the joy of a baby's birth, so children need to be taught what is appropriate and how to communicate the concern and love they feel and represent on behalf of the church. Of course, there are situations where children should not be included. Some people might not appreciate or want a child's visit. Some situations of acute grief or crisis might be frightening or overwhelming to a child or call for help beyond what a child can offer. There are many more situations, however, where a child's presence can be both appreciated and helpful. Children often enjoy the caring visit of another child when they are ill. Chronically ill and homebound people often value the inclusion of a child in a visiting team.

Including children in Christian care ministry provides several benefits: (1) children feel valued and valuable as contributing members of the church community, and they are; (2) children learn to care for others and understand people and relationships better; (3) children grow spiritually from serving; (4) adults learn to value the sensitive care children often bring; (5) adults recognize children's gifts, not just their needs; and (6) the adult and the child on the Christian care team develop a one-to-one relationship with one another that is often unique in the lives of both.

Here are ways to strengthen the role of children in Christian care.

• Teach children and youth how to visit sick and homebound members; be concrete and help them practice what to say and how to act.

• Encourage children to make a small gift or card to take on a visit.

• Encourage adult team members to make time to talk with the young person about the visit(s) they made, perhaps while sharing an ice cream cone or a soft drink at the end of the visit.

• Help children to make a card or telephone someone who is sick or has had a birthday, new baby, or death in the family.

• Have children adopt a "secret pal" (such as a homebound person) and write notes or reach out in other ways to that person.

There are other ways in which children can be included in the Christian care of the congregation. Mary Duckert suggests that even preschoolers can be involved in "disciple work," the work of being Jesus' disciples. Following the model of Luke 10 in which disciples were sent out two by two, children work in pairs along with an older member of the congregation on a project of ministry which no one can quite do alone, but that can be accomplished as they work together. This brings the joy of a shared activity, an opportunity to build relationships across the generations, and an activity to learn by doing ministry. For example, one congregation's preschoolers, with their ministry partners, prepare and send letters to welcome newborns and adoptees into the congregation.

The letters are often the first a child ever receives. Because they are done in part by preschoolers, they contain more illustration than printed messages. One such letter to a new baby said, "You're going to like it here. These are the things we like." It contained drawings and pictures of people, pizza, roses, and animals. Another group collects their outgrown picture books and sends them to mission churches where they can be shared with younger children (Duckert, 1991). Children may be paired with someone in the congregation who often prepares food to take to sick or homebound members. They can help prepare and deliver the meals.

Administration

Children can also participate in the decisions and business of the church. Asking them to share their time and energy to help make decisions communicates that we believe they belong and have much to offer. Many parents consult and involve their children far more in family decisions than their church does. Obviously, children need to be included as they are developmentally ready. Preschoolers and young school-age children may be present for church committee meetings, but usually only because their parents serve on the committee. Even so, they can be included in meaningful ways in the work of the committee, as the committee engages in projects or talks about the life of the church. A young child may be asked to draw a picture of the aspect of the church life which the committee is addressing. Then the picture can be used on a poster or in the church newsletter to communicate the work of the committee to the rest of the church body.

Older school-age children and youth can take active roles as committee members, particularly on committees whose work directly affects them. They can help to plan for the future as well as the present. It may be that a committee, after experiencing the participation of a young person, will find it helpful to include more than one child in their work. Children and youth of different ages will be able to participate and contribute in different ways.

Committee meetings need to be structured differently when they include children. Rather than assigning children to committees, first take time with adult members to discuss the reasons children need to be included in the administration of the church. Discuss questions and concerns about what including children in the business of the church might mean. Help committee members, particularly those who may be uncomfortable working with children, learn how they can listen to and talk with children. As a committee plans to include children in its work, some of the following suggestions may be helpful in working with children.

• Plan a slower pace, with careful, concrete explanations. "I will lead on slowly . . . according to the pace of the children" (Genesis 33:14 RSV);

• Listen to children and youth, and with your own attention and recognition, sensitize other committee members to the contributions of children;

• Find ways to use at least a part of children's suggestions;

• Use games to learn one another's names, to learn more about one another, to generate ideas for the committee's work, and to break meetings into segments of 30 minutes or less;

• Plan some hands-on activities related to what the committee is doing (e.g.:the worship committee can make a banner or write a responsive reading for the worship service; the social ministries committee can make an exhibit or poster about community opportunities for service; the building and grounds committee can plant a tree or paint nursery furniture together);

• Use small working groups to avoid long committee meetings;

• Encourage children to make drawings or in other ways provide reports to the church community about the work of the committee that can be included in the church newsletter or bulletin;

• Sing together to begin and/or end meetings;

• Meet early in the evening, perhaps over a potluck or fast-food meal, to avoid conflict with bedtimes;

• Meet more often and in shorter time segments;

• Be as sensitive to children's heavy homework nights and soccer team schedules as you are to adults' conflicting responsibilities when you choose meeting times.

You may find that implementing some of these suggestions will also help adults become more active, creative committee members. For example, when children show signs of fatigue or boredom during a meeting, they often are signaling that the adults also would work more creatively if the meeting were adjourned or the committee discussion were continued over a shared activity.

Children can also help with other work in the church community—serving tables for a church meal or a reception after the worship service, participating in work parties repairing hymnals or planting shrubbery. When they serve alongside adults, they have opportunities to deepen relationships and feel significant to the congregation. Children who have age-appropriate chores in their homes have healthier self-esteem, particularly if those chores are done alongside adult members of the family and contribute to the family's life. The same will be true of children who contribute to their church community.

Ministry

Children can be included in the ministry of the church and the work of the church for social justice. Age-graded missions education organizations have done an excellent job of involving children in ministry in their communities and beyond—organizing and leading a holiday party for children living in a shelter for homeless families, making special gifts for nursing home residents, and gathering Christmas-in-August gifts to be sent to missionaries. Children can also serve alongside adults in churchwide ministry projects, just as they do in the Christian care of the community.

Advocacy is not just an adult activity. Older children and youth have the ability to put themselves in the place of others who are suffering. They understand the hurt of children who do not have money for a school field trip or young people who hate school because they cannot read well. Children have a keen sense of fairness and justice. Children are aware of community and world issues and events. They worry about poverty, the ecology, and the fate of other people. Children and youth can be powerful advocates for other children. The church can be a place to act on their concerns.

Encouraging children to serve and be advocates for others helps them develop spiritually. They have learned that Jesus taught us to love our neighbors as ourselves. That teaching becomes a part of their lives when they experience love for their neighbors through actions. This has even greater meaning when it is ministry of the church which includes both children and adults. Churches can involve children in ministry and advocacy for social justice in the following ways.

• Ask children about problems in the world that most concern them, and help them find ways to address those problems; then, include those concerns and problems in the prayers, worship focus, and ministry activities of the congregation.
• Include issues of justice and the needs of others in Vacation Bible School and Sunday School; use banners, posters, and the drawings of children from these activities to lead the church in its emphasis on ministry and social justice.
• Organize an intergenerational group to study a social problem and find ways for your church to become involved in ministry to others and advocacy for justice for others.
• Include children and youth in congregational projects which address the needs of others (planning a Christmas toy sale for low-income parents, planning parties for children and families in a homeless shelter, sponsoring a homeless family, writing letters to congressional representatives about social justice issues, tutoring younger children in an after-school program).

Including children in these ways provides opportunities for adults to know children and for children to know adults. In addition to opportunities, however, many adults need to develop skills in communicating with children, if the opportunity for child-adult relationships is to become a reality. Just because adults were once children certainly does not mean that adults naturally know how to listen and talk with children.

KNOWING CHILDREN—TALKING, LISTENING, UNDERSTANDING

Learning to talk to children, listen to them, understand them, and encourage them to share their lives does not come easily for most people. Even those who are comfortable talking to teenagers may be very uncomfortable and unsure of their communication skills when talking to a four-year-old. Those who are comfortable with preschoolers may not be comfortable with adolescents. The truth of the matter is, many adults are afraid to try to relate to children and youth because they do not know how. When they have tried to reach out to a youngster, they have received in return a child's shy silence or a teen's uninterested shrug of the shoulders. What does an adult say to children after asking about school or commenting on how pretty or handsome they look in their Sunday clothes? Here are ways adults in a church community can learn to relate to children in their midst. The following general guidelines are not comprehensive, but they may help the adults in your congregation feel more comfortable with children.

1. Children experience the world differently than adults. Children have different ways of knowing about the world than adults do. Their understanding of the world is organized in different ways. For example, small children do not separate thoughts from actions. They think that if they have a thought, that thought will have an impact on the world around them. For example, if five-year-old Bob has hateful thoughts about his little sister, he may feel guilty when she falls and hurts herself. He may think that his hateful thoughts caused the injury. Imagine Bob's thoughts if an adult observes a bandage on her leg and jokingly asks Bob what he did to his sister! The response may be "nothing," and the adult may feel at a loss for how to pursue any further conversation with Bob. Bob may feel guiltier about his negative feelings toward his sister. He may miss the warmth and friendliness which the adult intended to communicate.

In order to understand children, then, we may need information that children cannot give us about their cognitive, physical, emotional, and social development. Adults who talk, work, or care for children need at least a brief review of child development. Many excellent resources help adults know how children grow and learn. Some of these resources are listed at the end of this chapter.

2. Children do not always understand that adults want to talk with them. Children learn early that some of their words and ideas can make adults anxious or upset, or that adults do not want to take the time to talk with them. They learn, therefore, not to talk about some things, and to make polite conversation. The extent of conversation between children and most adults is a response to such questions as, "How's school?" "Are you looking forward to summer vacation?" "Did you get your hair cut?" "Where did you get that pretty dress?" Children have learned that such questions are often polite conversation which seek only a one or two syllable response. They are ways that adults recognize the presence of children, perhaps a way of being courteous to parents, but which in fact block any further development of conversation between adult and child.

Other conversations between children and adults are usually in structured learning situations, such as school or Sunday School. Conversations in these settings are designed primarily to teach children particular information, not for deepening the relationship between adults and children. ("How do you think Noah felt when he stepped out of the ark?" "What does the rainbow mean?" "What does it mean to make a promise?") In these settings, adults ask questions to which they already know the answer. The questions test or help children to learn. Children often assume that adults always know (or think they know) the answers to the questions they ask. Thus, children easily fall into the role of answering adults' questions and then waiting to see if the adults think they are right or ask another question. Therefore, the pattern of question-and-answer develops between adults and children, which leaves adults often wondering what question to ask next to keep the conversation going. This pattern does not encourage mutual sharing. Here are some ways to encourage a child to share their thoughts and feelings.

- Ask open-ended questions. ("What was the best thing that happened to you this week?" instead of a yes-no question such as "Have you had a good week?")
- Give a child time to think about answers; don't rush.
- When a child gives a too-brief response for you to understand, admit your lack of understanding and ask for help. ("I'm afraid I don't understand. Let's imagine that I'm a kid smaller than you and you have to show me what you mean. How would you show me?" or "I have a hard time understanding. Let's pretend I'm a person from a faraway country and I don't know anything about school. Can you explain it to me?")
- Ask or comment on something that involves the child (what he watched on TV last night or what games he plays) instead of commenting on his clothes, how nice he looks or how pretty she is, or how tall he has grown. Children have little control over how they look; it may be hard for them to say much about their height or clothing. However, they may give you the whole plot of the TV show they watched!
- Rather than talking about how pretty or good a picture is which a child has drawn in Sunday School, comment on the qualities of

the picture. ("Look at all the colors you used.") Ask the child to tell you what she has drawn. In addition to telling a child or young person how well she sang or played an instrument, ask what kinds of music she likes best.

• Be willing to share your own thoughts and feelings about similar experiences you have had, keeping your stories short and relevant to the child's experiences. ("When I was your age, I didn't have a dog. My parents wouldn't let me. But I did have a rabbit, and when the rabbit died, I was very sad. I used to put flowers on its grave.")

3. Speak normally when talking with children. You don't have to speak loudly, slowly, or like a hyped-up children's television show to talk with children.

4. Use space to communicate both respect and affection. All of us need to feel loved and cherished by loving touches from others. Few adults, however, want to have people move inches from their faces to talk, tousle their hair, or pick them up! Children feel the same way. We communicate respect when we recognize that we earn the right to move close to one another. Because adults are bigger than children, we need to be particularly careful to offer touch only when the relationship invites it. Sometimes that happens when children move closer to us, inviting us to be close to them. Other times, we volunteer gestures which communicate affection to another, whether an adult or a child, such as a handshake, or a hand on the shoulder or arm.

In our world today, children are particularly confused by people who move too quickly and closely. Because of the justifiable fears and protectiveness of parents and teachers, most children have been warned to be wary of adults who want to touch them, especially in ways they do not want to be touched. Here are some suggestions for using the space between yourself and a child in ways that communicate both respect and affection.

- Sit down or kneel down so that you and a child can look at one another on the same level. Remember, however, that children are not used to adults doing this and that it lessens the distance between your face and the child's, so be careful to back away a little to retain some distance. This allows children to move toward you rather than wanting to back away.
- Keep your hands to yourself, particularly with children you do not know well. Allow children to give you the cues that it is OK to touch; they may gently touch you or lean against your arm. You may then respond with a touch to their arm or shoulder—or simply allow them to maintain or end the contact as they are comfortable.
- For children who feel safe with you, use gestures that communicate warmth, such as a hand on the shoulder or arm, or even a hug, not gestures that communicate adult/child differences in status, such as tousling their hair or patting their heads.

5. Be sensitive to the fact that children—and their parents—live in a world haunted by scary adults. Parents in our society live with the dark fear that their children will be sexually molested by an adult. They know that children most often become victims of people they know, not strangers. Consequently, many parents have communicated a wariness to their children, and they live in a constant state of alert to signs that another adult may be taking an unusual interest in their children. Be sensitive to their concerns. If you call and talk with a child on the telephone, take a moment to tell parents why you are calling. If you take time to talk privately with a child in a hallway or classroom at church, take a moment to say to a parent, "I enjoyed talking with Susan about her new school." If you are going to spend time with a child, tell the parents exactly what you are planning. Almost all parents are thrilled to have another adult recognize how special their child is; you simply need to let the parent know your friendly intentions.

6. Actions and physical presence communicate as loudly as words to children. Children feel special when an adult friend takes time to attend a musical recital, a ball game, or some other event in which they are participating. Presence communicates to a child: *I care enough about you to remember that this is a special time, and I want to take time to be here with you.*

Children need the ministry of their church during crisis times as much as their parents. A visit to a hospitalized child needs to include talking with the child, not just the worried parent. A child who has lost a pet, a sibling, or a grandparent often needs someone in addition to the parent to attend to his or her sense of loss. Going to a new school, feeling uncomfortable from or embarrassed by new orthodontic braces, winning or losing an athletic contest, or having an older brother or sister go off to college are significant events in the life of a child or young person. A brief visit or phone call can communicate: *I care about you.*

7. Children often communicate most effectively through actions and play. A relationship with a child needs to be a *doing* relationship, not just a *talking* relationship. Playing card games or board games, baking, doing a craft activity, taking a walk, playing tick-tack-toe on the disposable paper tablecloth during Wednesday night church suppers while waiting for the prayer meeting to begin—these are often the ways relationships with children are formed and deepened. Teenagers *open up* more when they are engaged in an activity rather than feeling expected to talk.

TAKING CHILDREN'S NEEDS SERIOUSLY

A congregation that includes children in its work and worship has a strong base for caring for the needs of children. Adults who seek out friendships with children, learn about the issues and problems which face them. In chapter 1, the Big Brother of Anthony, the ten-year-old who lives in poverty and shares church shoes with his brother, knows from firsthand experience the needs of children living in poverty. Making friends with children who live in poverty, or spend hours at home alone after school in front of the television, or have trouble in school teaches us about their needs and the needs of other children like them. Some congregations have all they can do to address the needs of the children in their midst. If a church is located in an urban area, the diversity of needs of children in our society may well be represented in the needs of the church's own children. Churches in affluent suburbs may have little contact with poor children, but the church members are deeply concerned about their children and issues of drugs, alcohol, teen pregnancy, and cultural violence.

Whether the needs of children are within our church walls, in the community which surrounds us, or in slums across town, congregations need to learn about those needs. Dieter Hessel suggests that education for social justice needs to heed four kinds of voices on social issues.

First, we need to hear from **children** themselves, especially those who are in need. Second, we need to hear from **professionals** who are trying to help children and their families. They are the professional staff of family support programs, family counseling centers, community agencies, and schools. Third, we need to hear from the **people who make the policies** which affect children and their families. This group includes state legislators who control funds for child health and education programs, television station managers who deal with commercials and scheduling of programming, community planners who determine where to put parks and playgrounds. They face their own pressures and dilemmas, and our advocacy in behalf of children will be more effective if we try to understand the issues from their perspective. Finally, we need to hear from **people who have studied the issues** which affect children but who are not being supported by programs which grow out of current government and social policies.

It is hard for a government employee to criticize the government agency which pays her salary or the teacher to criticize the school board's policy. A helpful resource on children's issues is the Children's Defense Fund, an independent research and advocacy organization that provides helpful perspectives, books, pamphlets, and newsletters (see the references at the end of chapter 3). Faculty members of universities and seminaries who teach child welfare, home economics, developmental psychology, education, or social work are also helpful sources of information.

When contacting a professional to address your church group, follow these suggestions for making the occasion as productive as possible.

• Tell the expert specifically why you are calling and what you want to know about.

• If the expert cannot help you, ask for suggestions of others whom you might call.

• Be clear at the outset if you have funds to offer in appreciation for the expert's time in preparation and presentation, or if you are not able to offer remuneration. Remuneration is not appropriate for elected public officials, but it is appreciated by professionals who are rendering your group a service as a consultant.

• Provide the expert with a list of specific questions your group would like help in answering, or specific objectives you would like the session to meet.

• Tell the expert about the people in your group—their gifts and relevant experiences, and what they have already learned or done with respect to the children's issue being addressed by the expert.

• Be sure that the expert understands what kind of action, if any, your group is considering based on what you are learning, so that the expert can make suggestions.

• Ask the expert to suggest written materials, videotapes, or other resources that might be helpful to your group.

Finding a community staff person, a state congressional representative or local government official, or a university professor to address a church group about a children's issue is a challenge. A far greater challenge, however, is to listen to the voices of children and their parents. They are the voices which bring home to us the concerns and needs of children as no other voices can. They bring life to the statistics and present the reality of complex issues.

We need children to help us understand not only the world "out there" but also the church itself. Sometimes we need to be advocates for children within the community of faith. For example, how might the programs of the church look to a child like Kathy who is only in our congregation every other week? She moves constantly between the households of her divorced parents. Programs which reward weekly attendance seem unjust and penalize children living in two households. Programs which are completed each session communicate: *We are happy to have you with us when you can be here. We want you to feel a part whether you can be here every week or not.*

One of the most difficult but most potentially powerful educational processes is arranging for adults to talk to children. Children can talk about what they do and how they feel when they are home alone after school. Children can describe their schools, their worries, what it is like to live in a poor single-parent family. Before asking children to talk about their experiences, be sure to ask permission from the parents. Because of confidentiality, clients in an agency's programs may not be available for interviewing by concerned church groups. Sometimes, however, they can write or tell their stories on tape, and identifying data can be changed. Hearing children's stories, visiting an agency, and talking with tutors, child-care workers, and other professional staff can galvanize your church group for action.

There is no substitute for firsthand experience. Church groups need to visit children in need if they are not a part of it on an everyday basis. For example, congregational groups who are considering advocacy for homeless families need to visit family shelters and talk to staff and residents. The chapters which follow make specific suggestions about ways your congregation can become acquainted with the issues that face children. Here are some general suggestions, however, for making such visits.

• Involve the agency director or appropriate program staff person in careful planning of the visit.

• Provide your group with basic information and brochures about the agency prior to the visit.

• Discuss basic guidelines for visitors, such as (1) being as unobtrusive as possible when they visit the site if clients are present, (2) not indicating knowledge of any client whom they may recognize unless the other speaks first, and (3) respecting the privacy of clients they may meet and keeping any information they learn about specific persons confidential.

• Take time to discuss afterward what they learned and how they felt (Guy, 1991, 53).

CARING FOR CHILDREN BY CARING FOR FAMILIES

We often find that the most caring, loving response to the issues which confront children may be to listen and respond to the needs of their parents. Many parents need friendship and support in order to care for their children effectively. We know, for example, that the abusive, neglectful parent is usually the parent who is isolated with little or no support from friends and family. To care for the parent is to care deeply and meaningfully for the parent's children.

In the past, parents had more support from friends and family for the task of nurturing children than they do today. Most mothers worked in the home and their friendships were neighborhood-centered. Children walked to the nearest school. Their families lived near one another in the same neighborhood. Churches were in neighborhoods, not across town. As a consequence, parents knew the parents of their children's friends, and those parents usually lived in the same neighborhood or rural community. Families knew families and shared some responsibility for child care with one another. Neighbors looked out for one another's children.

Radical changes have brought about a different world. With most parents working away from home, adult friendships are more likely to be based in work settings rather than in neighborhoods. Children may be transported to a distant school rather than walking to the neighborhood school. Schools are larger and more impersonal, with few links to other relationships in a child's life. Churches have become specialized. Members often drive across town to reach the congregation that meets their needs.

Extended families are smaller and more geographically scattered. Grandparents, aunts, and uncles are scarce, and most work outside the home, too. They may be unable to offer support and caregiving for youngsters and their parents. Parents today face the task of childrearing with much less involvement from neighbors, friends, grandparents, and siblings. If a neighbor down the street sees Tommy misbehaving, she is far less likely to march Tommy home or to call his parents. She does not know his parents and may fear their reaction if she interferes.

When a child comes home from school saying that "everybody else" is allowed to attend a concert or watch a certain television show, parents may not know any other parents of other children in their child's school with whom to confer. As a consequence, many parents feel alone with the responsibility for being all and doing all for their children. When parents are single or are stressed by poverty, unemployment, mental illness, or the special needs of a child, they may feel swamped.

The following chapters explore the issues which confront children and parents—inadequate preschool and after-school care, poverty, a failure of school and life opportunities, and chaotic family life. The chapters tell the stories of children and provide statistics of the social problems behind the stories. The chapters describe how people and churches reach out with care and love. They suggest ways you and your church may be able to respond.

Some of these responses are directed to the needs of children; others address the needs of parents. The goal is always to seek justice, to love kindness, and to walk humbly with God.

For the beauty of the earth,
For the glory of the skies,
For the children ev'rywhere,
With their sad or joyful cries,
God of All, to Thee we raise
This our hymn of grateful praise.

For the parents giving birth,
For the varied fam'ly ties,
For each child whose life of worth
May be missed by human eyes,
God of All, to Thee we raise
This our hymn of grateful praise.

For the hungry, homeless ones
Seeking life despite despair,
For the nations buying guns
While the children wait for care,
God of All, this plea we raise:
Help us change our hurtful ways.

Thanks for gifts the children bring:
Love and trust and open hands.
Help us give them songs to sing,
Meet their needs as love commands.
God of All, this prayer we raise:
Let us bring forth better days.

Tune: Dix: *For the Beauty of the Earth.*
Words: Virginia Sargent. Used by permission.

Resources for Learning about Child Development and Communicating with Children

Aleshire, Daniel. 1988. *Faithcare: Ministering to All God's People Through the Ages of Life*. Philadelphia: The Westminster Press.

The ways a church can help children to grow in faith as they develop cognitively, emotionally, and socially.

Blazer, Dolores A. (Ed.) 1989. *Faith Development in Early Childhood*. Kansas City: Sheed & Ward.

Describes the faith development of children.

Hendricks, William L. 1980. *A Theology for Children*. Nashville: Broadman Press.

A guide for effectively teaching children about God.

Lester, Andrew. 1985. *Pastoral Care with Children in Crisis*. Philadelphia: Westminster.

A guide for providing pastoral care to children. Practical guidelines for both pastors and lay persons in communicating with and caring for children in crises.

Rowatt, G. Wade. 1990. *How to Talk with Teenagers*. Nashville: Broadman.

A guide for parents and other adults who want to communicate more effectively with teenagers and guide them in coping with everyday problems.

Shelly, Judith Allen. 1982. *The Spiritual Needs of Children*. Downers Grove, IL: InterVarsity Press.

Explores the faith development of children.

Waldrop, Sybil. 1985. *Guiding Your Child Toward God*. Nashville: Broadman.

Describes the development of preschoolers year-by-year and how parents (and preschool teachers and group leaders) can guide them toward God in everyday experiences and interaction.

Resources for Including Children in Church Life

Duckert, Mary. 1991. *New Kid in the Pew: Shared Ministry with Children*. Louisville: Westminster/John Knox Press.

A practical guide for structuring children's ministries in a congregation in ways that children and adults are discipled through shared worship, Christian education, ministry, and celebration. Liberally illustrated with examples from the lives of parents and their children.

Guy, Kathleen. 1991. *Welcome the Child: A Child Advocacy Guide for Churches.* Children's Defense Fund, 122 C Street, NW, Washington, DC 20001.
Contains resources for planning a Children's Day in worship, and for guiding a church congregation in child advocacy.

Heusser, Phyllis. 1985. *Children as Partners in the Church.* Valley Forge: Judson Press.
Contains suggestions for including children in worship.

McGinnis, Kathy, and McGinnis, Jim. 1983. *Parenting for Peace and Justice.* Maryknoll, NY: Orbis.
The authors describe their own experiences and that of other families in making justice issues a part of their family life. Suggestions for including children in advocacy are easily adaptable to the church congregation.

United Church of Canada. 1989. *A Place for You: Toward the Integration of Children Into the Life of the Church.* The United Church of Canada, Division of Mission in Canada, 85 St. Clair Avenue, East, Toronto, Ontario M4T1M8.
Resource notebook for congregational committees and groups interested in finding ways to integrate children of all ages into the worship, administration, and Christian care of the congregation. Includes intergenerational activities and other practical suggestions for studying the role of children in the life of the church.

3

Children Whom No One Minds

I cry aloud to the Lord;
I lift up my voice to the Lord for mercy.
I pour out my complaint before him;
before him I tell my trouble.

When my spirit grows faint within me,
it is you who know my way.
In the path where I walk
men have hidden a snare for me.

Look to my right and see;
no one is concerned for me.
I have no refuge;
no one cares for my life.

I cry to you, O Lord;
I say, "You are my refuge,
my portion in the land of the living."
Listen to my cry,
for I am in desperate need (Psalm 142:1-6a NIV).

Many children today can say with the psalmist: *I have no refuge; no one cares for me.* Ten-year-old David, whom you met in chapter 1, is such a child. For hours after school each day, he is alone with the responsibility for his eight-year-old brother and six-year-old sister. Other children, too young to consider leaving alone, are parked in child-care arrangements which barely meet their needs for physical safety and do not attend to their needs for nurture and stimulation. They seem similar to automobiles in a parking garage, stored until their owners return at the end of the day. Desperate parents are doing the best they can to support their children, frustrated that they cannot find better care for their children while they work.

ONE CHILD'S STORY

Patricia wakes her baby, Peggy, and two-year-old, Jonathan, at 6:00 A.M. to feed and dress them. They must leave the house by 7:00 in order to be at the baby-sitter's house by 7:30, so that Patricia can be at work by 8:00. Patricia leaves work at 5:00 in the afternoon and reverses the trip. She and the children arrive home at 6:00 P.M., 12 hours after they began their day. Patricia then prepares supper, cleans house, bathes the children, washes clothes, pays bills, and all the other tasks single parents bear alone.

Patricia worries about her children. She knows that her sitter cares for a baby of her own and two other preschoolers. Caring for two babies and three preschoolers is a lot of responsibility. Peggy is a quiet baby, and Patricia is suspicious that because Peggy doesn't demand much attention, she gets almost none. When Patricia picks up the children, Peggy is always sitting in a wind-up swing, swinging quietly in front of the television blaring sitcom reruns or the evening news. Often, her diaper is dirty. Patricia wonders how long she has been sitting there, but she is afraid to ask the sitter, afraid it will sound like she is being critical. She is afraid the sitter might take it out on the children.

Patricia worries about what the children's day is like. She would like to drop in sometime to see what is happening, but she cannot leave her job just to visit the baby-sitter's home for no reason. Besides, it is the best she can do right now. She dreams of placing the children in a day-care center where they would have activities to stimulate their development, but child-care centers are expensive. Patricia is in the midst of a divorce and receives no child support. She has a minimum wage job; she has applied for child-care assistance from a state program for low-income families, but there is a long waiting list.

The Facts About Child Care

Why don't parents just stay home and care for their own children? Some Christian leaders have stated emphatically that mothers should stay home "where they belong" and then there would not be a child-care problem. Dolores Curran, a prominent parent educator, encountered a picketer outside a church child-care conference with a sign reading, *Would Mary have put Jesus in day care?* Curran says that the sign caused her to think. What would have happened if Joseph had not believed the angel appearing to him in a dream telling him to take Mary as his wife despite her strange pregnancy? Mary might have been sent away in shame, to find herself in a strange town, solely responsible for supporting herself and her baby. She might well have turned to her synagogue for help, hoping for the kind of loving, faith-based care for her child that the people of God can give (Curran, 1991). Arguing that parents ought to stay home and provide care for their own children does not address the plight of many families who, for many reasons, need child care. As Jesus said, caring for the little ones is caring for Him.

Single parents work so that they and their children can survive. Many people believe that welfare makes it possible for single women who have no financial support to stay home and care for their children, at least while the children are preschoolers. Originally, AFDC (Aid to Families with Dependent Children) was designed to do just that. AFDC is the welfare program which provides funds to impoverished families with dependent children. But living on current levels of AFDC grants is next to impossible. In the past 15 years, inflation has doubled the cost of living, yet the average AFDC monthly allotment for a mother with two children has risen only $50. In 1990, the average maximum AFDC monthly benefit for a family of three was $367; in five states, it was less than $200 (CDF, 1991, 26). Few of us would want to try to raise two children on $367 per month, much less $200. Mothers work, then, because they need the income and benefits (such as medical insurance) that come with working. In Europe, where longer maternity leaves are available, there are very few infants in out-of-home care, even in countries where a higher overall percentage of women are working than in the United States. In the United States, mothers of small children often work because they must.

Some families live on AFDC grants. Few choose to do so. Many women receiving welfare benefits say they would work if adequate, affordable child care were available. In a 1986 study of welfare participants, nearly two out of three said that child care was their primary problem in seeking and keeping a job (Guy, 1991, 65). As difficult as it is to live on the small income AFDC provides, it is even more difficult for these women to find jobs that pay enough for them to be able to afford adequate child care as well as money to pay rent and buy food.

Many two-parent families need both parents to work. Single-parent families are not alone in the need to place children in day care while parents work. In many families, both spouses must work for them to survive, not just to have extra money. In 1989, the House Select Committee on Children, Youth, and Families reported that in two-parent homes, 60 percent of employed mothers had husbands who earned less than $20,000 annually (Zigler, 1990, 243). Between 1973 and 1989, the average wages of hourly workers (adjusted for inflation) fell by 29 percent among men younger than 25. During the same time period, wages for men age 25 and older fell by 19 percent (CDF, 1991, 24). Fathers of young children find their earning power cut dramatically compared with what fathers of young children earned 15 years ago. Consequently, families need two incomes. Fifteen years ago, many women worked so that their families could have the extras—a vacation, a new refrigerator. Now both spouses need to work to pay the rent and to buy groceries and clothing for the family.

As a consequence of these factors, more than half of all preschool children are now cared for outside their home while their parents work. More than half of all American women with babies younger than one year are in the labor force (CDF, 1991, 38). Three out of four school-age children live in families in which both parents work outside the home (CDF, 1991, 38; Seligson, Fersh, Marshall, & Marx, 1990, 324). Researchers estimate that two out of three preschool children will have mothers in the work force by 1995. In the past, grandparents or other relatives provided care for working mothers. The amount of care available from relatives, however, is declining. More and more parents find that their relatives either live too far away or are in the work force themselves and thus cannot help with child care. Some relatives simply do not want to be full-time caregivers for young children.

Many children need quality child care because of the deprivation which comes with poverty or because of family problems. High quality care is important for all children, but it is critical for poor children. Research confirms that good child care can help make up for a variety of deprivations children suffer when they grow up in poverty. In addition, whether poor or not, children from stressed and disorganized homes, or children who have parents who are mentally ill or addicted to drugs or alcohol, need quality day care to survive their home circumstances. Stable, emotionally satisfying, nurturing relationships with caregivers outside their families can make all the difference for these children.

Unfortunately, too many children are deprived at home, and then, because of the scarcity of quality, affordable day care, they don't receive the care they need away from home either. The children who are most likely to have stable, nurturing home lives are also the children most likely to have the best child care, because their parents have the resources to seek it out and pay for it. Even so, good care is not available in some communities, even for the children of parents who can afford it.

Quality child care for infants and preschoolers is not available for the children who need it most. Child care is a triple problem for many parents. First, it simply is not available. Second, when available, it often is inadequate or substandard. Finally, if available and adequate, it is often unaffordable. A survey of child-care costs for one-year-olds in 1990 reported that the average cost of full-time care in a child-care center ranged from almost $4,000 per year in Dallas, Texas, to almost $11,000 in Boston, Massachusetts. In Dallas, a single mother who works full time at the minimum wage would have to spend almost half her income to pay for infant child care for one child (CDF, 1991, 42). Low-income families often have to find the cheapest child care available, even though, like Patricia, they worry about what it is doing to their children.

> A few years ago in a neighborhood near Chicago, 47 youngsters were discovered being cared for in a basement by only one adult. It's unlikely that any of the parents of those children were happy about the arrangement, but, at $25 a week, the program cost only one-third as much as most child care in the community (Guy, 1991, p. 65).

Middle and upper middle class parents are more likely to be able to pay for better quality care for their children. Working class and poor families, however, have few or no good options. More child-care programs are available for preschool children than for babies, but many of these programs operate only part of the day. Young children often have to be picked up and dropped off to more than one caregiver, making it difficult to provide security and stability in their lives.

Government subsidies have helped in limited ways, paying the child-care costs for only some of the poor children who are eligible for it. Poor parents who cannot get subsidized care have to make the difficult choice between leaving their jobs or placing their children in risky, substandard care situations. When child-care arrangements fail and desperate parents fear losing their jobs, some parents have left their children at home alone.

Linda Grant lived in Dade County, Florida, with her children, three-year-old Anthony and four-year-old Maurice. Although she worked to support her children, her income was so low that she could not afford to pay for child care. Since she qualified for government assistance, she put her name on Florida's waiting list for child-care support—a list that included 22,000 other names.

Linda was told that it might be two years before she could expect government help. Meanwhile, she depended on friends and relatives to care for the boys while she worked. Some days, her arrangements fell through and, afraid of losing her job, she felt she had to go on to work and leave the boys alone. On one such day, Anthony and Maurice climbed into a seemingly cozy place—a clothes dryer—to look at a magazine. When they shut the door, the dryer started, and they tumbled and burned to death (Guy & Smith, 1988, p. 25).

Many young children are cared for in family day-care homes. About one-fourth of the care of preschoolers takes place in family day-care homes (CDF, 38). In family day-care homes, people care for a few children, often including their own, in the less formal setting of the caregiver's home. Patricia's children are cared for in a family day-care home. Some of these homes are licensed by state agencies, but many are not. Some provide very good care; others are abysmal. Several states still allow a single family day-care provider to care for five or more infants and toddlers. Yet child development experts recommend no more than three or four infants per caregiver. Many parents prefer family day-care homes because, in some cases, they:

- are less expensive than a child-care center;
- offer flexible hours (such as evening or early morning hours for shift workers);
- have a smaller number of other children in care;
- provide the consistency of a single caregiver, with whom the infant or child can have a close relationship;
- are located near home, requiring less commuting time;
- provide care for siblings together, including young school-age children who may come to the home of the family home-care provider after school;
- are more likely to accept a child who is mildly ill;
- will accept a child with special needs.

Care before and after school and during school holidays is difficult for many families. In many American communities, children are dismissed from school at 2:30 P.M., three or more hours before most parents can arrive home from work. Although some communities have after-school activity programs available in the school, community centers, churches, or child-care centers, many more do not. Parents are on their own to figure out after-school arrangements, which may mean children are loose on the streets or idle in front of the television. A study in the mid-1980s found that at least 2 million American children between the ages of 5 and 13 take care of themselves after school. One study of six rural communities showed that by the third grade (age 9), one child in ten cared for himself or herself some days after school, and four in ten were cared for by older brothers and sisters (CDF, 1991, 38).

A smash hit at the movie theater in early 1990, the movie *Home Alone* told the story of a young boy whose family went to Europe for a Christmas holiday and accidentally left him at home. For days, while his mother desperately tried to fly home to him through blizzards and other insurmountable odds, the young boy prepared his own meals, single-handedly fended off would-be robbers, and quite successfully cared for himself, although he felt lonely and frightened after the initial fun of doing what he wanted wore thin. The movie captured the imaginations of both adults and children; adults could identify with the helpless desperation of parents, and children were enthralled with the ability of one of their own to cope so successfully—all alone. The movie touched a nerve of American families who too often feel inept at providing care and hope that their young children can cope on their own. The unrealistic events in the movie, however, also suggest how unrealistic this hope is.

Our society does not value quality child care. The way we value children is reflected in the incomes of child-care workers; 87 percent of family day-care providers and 50 percent of all child-care workers receive earnings less than the poverty level (Schorr, 209). Poor pay and lack of training communicates the lack of value society attaches to this demanding work. In stark contrast, countries such as France subsidize quality child care for all children, and child-care workers are treated and paid as professionals (Schorr, 1988). As a consequence of low salaries and the highly demanding work, turnover among child-care workers in the United States is higher than in any other occupation. Consequently, many children go from caregiver to caregiver with very little stability (Schorr, 1988, 209).

Child care should be considered more than a place to park children while parents work. Quality child-care costs. Young children need to be cared for in small groups with adequate numbers of caregivers to ensure individualized attention and nurturing relationships between adults and children. Children need security and predictability which come from being able to count on the same caregivers. Turnover in child-care staff hurts children. Staff need training to meet the special needs of the children in their care. Children need facilities which are safe and which encourage and stimulate them to grow and learn.

CHILD CARE IN YOUR COMMUNITY

The kind of care available for preschool and school-age children varies widely from community to community. As an advocate for children, find out about the care children receive in your community. First, talk with people who know about child care for preschool and school-age children in the neighborhoods of your community. The following people may be helpful:

- the director of a local child-care center;
- the director of a Head Start program in your elementary school;
- Child Care Information and Referral staff (look in the telephone directory under Child Care);
- the child-care regulatory agency of the State Department of Social or Human Services (This agency has information about policies for child-care providers, statistics for your area, waiting lists for subsidized care for poor children, etc.);
- a local member of the National Council of Churches Ecumenical Child Care Network (Contact their office in New York for the name of people in your community. Their phone number is (212) 870-3342);
- a child development or early childhood education professor in a local community college, university, or seminary.

When you think you have an overall picture of child care in your community, learn about child care from the perspective of your community's children and their parents. Here are some ideas.
- Talk with parents in your church who have infants and preschool children in care outside their homes. Ask parents of school-age children what kinds of arrangements they have made

for the care of their children and any concerns they may have. Ask parents whose children are in different kinds of child care to serve on a panel.

- Talk to children in your Sunday School and missions programs. Ask children in self-care to tell you what they do after school and on school holidays. How do they spend their time? What rules do they have to follow? (Explain to parents why you are asking questions!)
- Talk to the principal or counselor of the elementary school. What do children with working parents do after school? Ask if there is help for children from poor families.
- Visit child-care centers and after-school programs in your community, especially those which serve poor and working-class families. Following the guidance of the experts you have consulted, try to visit a center that has few resources as well as one that has many resources for caring for children. Talk with staff about their waiting lists and their concerns about child care in your community.
- Locate several family day-care homes in your community. Call the providers and ask if you can talk with them about their services and their concerns. Explain that your church is looking for ways to help caregivers. Ask them to tell you about what they enjoy about their work, what the stressors are, and what they need.

As you talk with children, parents, and professionals, you form a picture of the kind of care available to children in your community. You will find some important ways your church can help.

WHAT CHURCH GROUPS AND
CONGREGATIONS CAN DO

Churches have taken the leadership in advocating and providing better care for preschool and school-age children. Your church may be one of those congregations that has taken an active role in providing child care, or you may be considering ways that you can be involved in caring for children. If you do not have the resources or facilities to provide weekday care for children, there are other ways you can advocate and support better care for children.

Provide an after-school or full-day child-care program in your church. If your church does not have the resources to provide such a program, cooperate with other community churches to develop a community ministry which can provide after-school and/or full-day child care.

The organization which provides the most child-care centers in our country is not the government. It isn't KinderCare. It is the churches of the Southern Baptist Convention (Freeman, 1986). Southern Baptist churches sponsor 4,000 child-care centers. They are followed by Roman Catholics, United Methodists, and Presbyterians. The top 19 organizations which provide child-care centers are all church denominations. Over 20,000 early childhood programs are housed in church facilities in this country. About one out of four of these centers offers reduced fees for poor children (Neugebauer, 1991). For every child in Sunday School on Sunday morning, there are eight children in a church-housed child-care center on Monday morning (Freeman, 1986, 27).

Your church may already offer care for children. If so, you may find that there are ways you can help strengthen the care that is offered and find ways your church can better serve children who need it most. Because church programs often earn reputations for providing the best care available for children, they often fill up with middle-class children whose parents are attracted to the quality of the program. Consequently, they may have little room for poor children whose parents are not able to pay full fees. Your group may be able to help your church's center offer scholarships and reserve slots for children with the greatest need.

The Head Start program, a highly successful preschool program for disadvantaged three- to five-year-olds, has been operating for 25 years. The program ensures that children receive the supportive services they need to be ready to succeed in school. It also provides family counseling and referral for parents who need extra help. Churches have been strong advocates for full funding of Head Start programs; many churches house Head Start programs.

If your church is not able to provide a full-day child-care program for infants and preschoolers or a Head Start program, you may be able to offer an after-school program for school-age children. If you already offer preschool child-care services, an after-school program may be an additional ministry you will want to consider. Child-care centers and after-school programs touch the lives of children and parents who otherwise would have no contact with a church community. They provide opportunities for us to minister in a significant way to basic family needs, and in the process, to communicate through caring relationships the love of Jesus Christ.

Do you remember David, Shawn, and Missy from chapter 1? The Baptist church in their neighborhood began offering an after-school program for children. The church offers a sliding fee scale based on family income so David's mother pays only $10 per week for her children to be picked up each day at school by the church van and cared for until she calls for them before 6:00 P.M. The van makes return trips to pick up children who are participating in after-school activities. The program is staffed by a full-time director, two part-time teachers, volunteers from the church's senior citizens group, and a few high school students. The program provides a snack after school and time to do homework. Each day there is quiet time to talk to friends, read, or play games. Woven throughout the program are learning experiences related to

Bible stories and Christian values. In addition, there is plenty of opportunity for outdoor sports and games, including swimming at the community pool.

David, Shawn, and Missy enjoy the friendships with other children, the contact with loving adults, the fun, and the security of feeling safe until their mother comes for them. David's mother is relieved by the good care her children are receiving. She appreciates conversations with caregivers about her children and her own needs as a single parent. The after-school program is offering several seminars for single parents at the church on Sunday evenings, and she plans to go. She thinks of the church as a place where people know her and care for her and her children.

Organize a network of family child-care providers. Many poor children are in family day-care homes and the homes of friends or relatives (Frankel, 1991). These children particularly need experiences which will help them to have a healthy start in school. Family child-care providers provide much of the care for young children, much of it loving and sensitive to children's needs, but they often are isolated and working for dreadfully low wages. Some churches are organizing networks of family child-care providers as a way of ministering both to the needs of the family child-care providers and to the children in their care. Your church might provide the following resources for family child-care providers in your community:

- a time and a place for family child-care providers to gather and share their experiences (perhaps while they watch their children play on the church or community playground or participate in an activity program sponsored by the church);
- seminars and training programs on topics relevant to family child care (e.g., first aid and emergency care of infants and young children, child development, nutrition, positive discipline, children's self-esteem, and faith development);

- a resource library of books, literature, and videotapes on topics relevant to family child care;
- a resource center of toys, videotapes, books and other supplies to loan to children;
- a co-op for purchasing at bulk rates art supplies and other materials used in family child care;
- the opportunity to employ an instructor for swimming, dance, or gymnastic classes for children in family child care;
- the opportunity for family child-care providers to speak with a united voice, writing or calling state and federal government officials in behalf of subsidies for low-income families and other issues which affect family child care;
- transportation for a special outing to a children's museum, swimming pool, or special event.

In Miami, the National Council of Jewish Women and the Kiwanis Club collaborated to raise money for a resource van. Inside the van was designed to resemble a child-care center. The van is staffed by an early education specialist who visits the homes of family child-care providers in the poorest neighborhoods of Black and Latino children, those homes with the least resources and support. The visits relieve the providers' isolation and provide them with training and new ideas. The specialist provides children with learning activities and an outing (CDF, 1991, 52-53). A church or community ministry could offer a similar program, perhaps as part of a family child-care provider network program.

Encourage state and federal legislation for child care for preschoolers and school-age children and monitor child-care programs in your community. If you do not have the resources for developing a child-care program in your church or community or a network of family child-care providers, you can still effectively advocate quality care for children. In churches all across the country, advocates for children have been working together for years to bring the critical needs for child care to the attention of the nation. They have written letters, called congressional representatives, and supported organizations lobbying the government to take a role in providing better care for all children.

Consequently, Congress passed a comprehensive child care legislation package in 1990, the Child Care and Development Block Grant and the amendments to Title IV-A of the Social Security Act ("At-Risk Child Care") (CDF, 1991). The legislation provides money for the states to make child care available, better, and more affordable for poor families. The majority of the money will go to poor parents. They receive vouchers to help pay for the child care of their choice. They can choose relatives, family day-care providers, church-housed child-care centers, or private centers. Vouchers can be used only to pay for care from providers who meet minimal requirements and are licensed. The rest of the money will be used to expand child-care services for other children, to provide care for school-age children (before and after school and during holidays), to strengthen quality and safety standards, and to improve caregiver salaries. Child advocates, with their letters and telephone calls, brought the needs of "the least of these" to the attention of the nation and provided the energy and support for government action. Many children will benefit from their efforts.

Children still need advocates to ensure that they receive the care they need. The money Congress made available to fund the legislation is not enough to do all that it is supposed to do. Congress needs to fund what it has legislated. Legislators need to be encouraged to provide more funds for children. Advocates for children need to keep an eye on the programs which develop in their own state. They need to express appreciation for congressional representatives who make sure that the intentions of federal legislation are carried out. The Children's Defense Fund provides current information which child advocates can use to stay informed about child-care issues in the states and nation.

The success of the new legislative package also depends upon quality child care becoming available through church and private child-care centers and family care homes. New centers need to be started. Loving adults need to be encouraged and supported in the ministry of providing child care. Child advocates need to monitor the kinds of care available in their communities to be sure that children are receiving the best care possible.

SEEKING JUSTICE, LOVING KINDNESS, WALKING HUMBLY WITH GOD

Justice calls for all children to have the kind of care that enables them to grow into trusting, faithful people, developing the gifts and abilities that God gave them.

"Loving kindness" is caring enough to ask school-age children what their lives are like when they are not in school, taking seriously their fears about being alone at home, being sensitive to David's wish to be able to play with his friends instead of caring for his younger siblings while his mother works. Different children and different families have different needs for care. Knowing the statistics about school-age children home alone and infants and toddlers in substandard care calls us to seek justice. Knowing David's burden and listening to Patricia's worries help us to reach out in care that is sensitive to individual needs.

The problems seem too big for us. We cannot solve them all alone. We pray for guidance and humbly seek God in our care for children, and we join with child advocates in churches all across the nation. Together, small voices make a loud chorus. That is what brought about the promise of change with the 1990 legislation package. Together, we can work toward the goal of child care in which babies do not sit idly in swings for hours, ten-year-old boys do not bear the responsibility for younger siblings for hours after school, and child-care centers do not exist where children are abused or simply ignored.

Background research and statistics for this chapter come from the Children's Defense Fund, especially *The State of America's Children 1991*.

Resources

Children's Defense Fund, 122 C Street, NW, Washington, DC 20001. The Ecumenical Child Care Network, National Council of the Church of Christ in the USA, 475 Riverside Drive, Room 572, New York, NY 10115-0050.

This network of church-sponsored child-care programs and providers shares ideas, resources, and support. The network distributes a helpful newsletter to its members.

Freeman, Margery (Ed.). 1986. *Called to Act: Stories of Child Care Advocacy in our Churches*. Child Advocacy Office, National Council of the Churches of Christ in the USA, 475 Riverside Drive, Rm. 472, New York, NY 10115.

This booklet tells the story of the various ways in which different churches in different places have responded to the needs for child care in their communities. It provides suggestions for organizing the church community and for advocating for children.

Freeman, Margery (Ed.) 1987. *Helping Churches Mind the Children: A Guide for Church-housed Child Day Care Programs*. New York: National Council of the Churches of Christ in the United States.

As the title states, this book provides guidance in developing a child day-care program.

National Association for Family Day Care. 725 15th Street, NW, Suite 505, Washington, DC 20005-2109.

A quarterly publication for family day-care providers.

Lindner, Eileen W., Mattis, Mary C., and Rogers, June R. 1983. *When Churches Mind the Children*. Ypsilanti, MI: High/Scope Press.

This book reviews the practical issues and concerns churches need to address in providing child-care programs.

4

Children in Poverty

Is not this the fast that I choose:
to loose the bonds of wickedness,
to undo the thongs of the yoke,
to let the oppressed go free,
and to break every yoke?
Is it not to share your bread with
the hungry,
and bring the homeless poor into
your house . . . ?
Then you shall call, and the Lord
will answer;
you shall cry, and he will say,
Here I am. . . .
If you pour yourself out for the
hungry
and satisfy the desire of the
afflicted,
then shall your light rise in the
darkness
and your gloom be as the
noonday.
And the Lord will guide you
continually (Isa. 58:6-11a RSV).

Poverty underlies the family struggles and hurts in the lives of most of the children you met in earlier chapters—Ben, the teenager lost in the chaos of a family ravaged by unemployment, alcoholism, and violence; Anthony, the child of a poor single mother who shares one pair of shoes with his brother; Darlene and Robert, the homeless teenaged mother and her two-year-old son; David and his younger brother and sister, home alone while their mother works at a minimum wage job to support them. Poverty saps a family's ability to cope with the ordinary and extraordinary crises of caring for one another.

Children are now the poorest age group in the United States. In the US, 40 percent of all poor people are children. One out of every four American preschoolers lives below the poverty line (Popenoe, 1990, 42).

ONE CHILD'S STORY

Eight months ago, David was laid off from his job in an automobile parts factory in Indiana due to production cutbacks. At age 24, David had been employed at the factory for two years and was one of the first to lose his job. It was the first good job he had had since he graduated from high school. Last year, he and his wife, Sharla, bought a modest three bedroom home when Sharla was expecting their second child. They chose the home in a nice suburban neighborhood as a good place to raise their children.

After the layoff, David was unable to find anything other than temporary employment. The combination of sporadic pay for occasional jobs plus unemployment benefits did not cover their mortgage, car payment, groceries, and other expenses. Their baby has asthma, and the medical bills for medication and frequent doctor visits are a steady drain on their meager resources. Neither David nor Sharla has a college degree, and with high unemployment rates in their community, the future seemed bleak. They were unable to pay the mortgage and lost their home. With no other place to turn, they packed their few remaining belongings into their station wagon and drove to St. Louis, where they and their two children moved into the second bedroom of David's parents' small home. David was humiliated to have to return to his parents' home as a young adult who is supposed to be responsible for his family, but there seemed to be no other choice. Although they understand David and Sharla's dilemma, David's parents feel cramped by having four other people in their home—including two preschoolers—and frightened about how long they can support David's family and meet their own expenses.

The two-year-old, Amanda, has shown signs of the strain; she has become clinging and unwilling to have her mother out of her sight. She has returned to wearing diapers after being toilet trained. The adults in the family are often cross and unhappy, and there is no safe place outside to play and no place indoors which is out of the way. David and Sharla find themselves arguing and increasingly alienated from one another as they try to find some way out of their present troubles; they don't know where to turn.

THE FACTS ABOUT CHILD POVERTY

David and Sharla's two children exemplify child poverty in the United States today, just as do the children of a mother working at a minimum wage job whose marriage ended in divorce, and the child of a single teenager struggling to survive on welfare while she tries to finish high school. The image we have of child poverty is that of a black child born to a single, teenaged mother living on welfare in an urban slum, yet only one in 1,000 poor children fits this picture (CDF, 1991, 22). Children of young married couples struggling to get on their feet comprise a significant proportion of child poverty. Whatever their particular situation, children in poverty live in desperate circumstances, and they suffer. Sidel has observed that statistics are simply people with the tears washed off (Sidel, 1986).

What is child poverty?
The US federal government defines poverty by relating income and family size. For example, in 1992, the government defined

families as poor if a family of two had an annual income of less than $9,190, if a family of three had an annual income of less than $11,570, if a family of four had an annual income of less that $13,950 and so on (CDF Reports: March 1992, 11). The poverty lines are changed each year by the change in the Consumer Price Index so they represent the same purchasing power for a family from year to year.

An income equal to or above the government-defined poverty level, however, does not guarantee that a family can meet its essential needs. The federal government's definition of poverty fails to take into account high housing and utility costs in some areas of the country, or the high cost of health care for families with chronic health problems, small children, and no insurance. It also does not consider child-care costs for working parents, which may take half or more of the earnings of many families with minimum wage jobs.

Many children live in families which are not just poor, but desperately poor. In 1989, 41 percent of all poor children were in families whose incomes were less than half the poverty line. A family of three people—father, mother, and child, or parent and two children—had to live on less than $412 per month for food, housing, medical care, clothing, transportation, and all the other expenses of living (CDF, 1991, 24). Clearly, these families were having to make such difficult choices as whether to eat or to get a child needed medical care.

Why are so many children living in poverty in the richest nation in the world?

Children are poor because their parents are poor. In earlier centuries, destitute families were sent to the poorhouse where they worked for their meager food and housing; their children were often taken away and placed in institutions or indentured as servants to middle-class or wealthy families. It was assumed that poverty was caused by laziness, immorality, poor family management, or squandering the family's resources on alcohol; in short, parents who could not provide economically for their children were not fit to be parents.

Our understanding of poverty has changed. No longer is poverty a justifiable rationale for removing children from the care of their parents. Parents may be loving, good parents, but still unable to provide adequate incomes to support their families. Parents and their children are poor because of many different circumstances.

•Mothers are trying to support their children on their own. More than half of all children born today will spend part or all of their childhood in a one-parent home, usually the home of their mother. In 1989, 52 percent of all poor families were headed by a single woman, almost double the percentage of female-only heads of households 30 years ago (CDF, 1991, 25). Women are on their own with their children primarily because of rising divorce rates. The proportion of births to unmarried women has also been increasing dramatically.

Many women find it difficult or impossible to pull their family out of poverty on their own. Most married couples in our society find it necessary for both parents to be employed in order to support their families; obviously, women on their own do not have the benefit of a second wage in the family. In addition, women generally earn far less than men—on the average, about 30 percent less. Many absent fathers fail to provide financial support to help care for their children; only one out of four women and their children receive the full annual amount of child support the court has ordered the father to pay (CDF, 1991, 27); one out of four receive no support from the absent father. Fathers who do contribute pay an average of 6 to 10 percent of their income to help with the care of their children, an amount far short of the actual costs of raising a child (Fletcher, 1989, 415).

•Parents cannot find work. Nearly half of all poor women who support their children alone have not finished high school. Limited education predicts poverty. These mothers have difficulty finding jobs. When they find jobs, the jobs usually include little on-the-job training and opportunity for advancement. Young families are the first to suffer when unemployment rates are high; they are the first to lose their jobs.

•Government programs designed to help poor families obtain jobs often miss their mark because of inadequate funding or short-sighted goals. Ten years ago, government assistance helped nearly one in five families with children escape poverty. Today, such programs successfully reach only one in ten families (CDF, 1991, 25). Too often, job training programs focus on moving people into jobs as quickly as possible, rather than helping them develop solid, marketable skills.

•Income support to families with children through AFDC (Aid to Families with Dependent Children) leaves families far below the poverty level. The AFDC program serves as the only safety net for children whose parents cannot support them financially because of death, disability, or absence of one or both parents. The AFDC safety net is too low to break the fall of families into poverty, however. The average AFDC benefit for a family is less than half the current poverty level—$367 a month for a family of three (CDF, 1991, 26). Unlike the poverty level, AFDC grants are not indexed to consumer prices, so that they do not keep pace with inflation. In constant dollars, the average maximum benefit has fallen 37 percent since 1970 (Plotnick, 1989, 525). AFDC currently provides less than four dollars per day to support a child. All across the country, AFDC benefits are so low that it is virtually impossible for parents to find even the most modest of rental housing for their families.

Food stamps provide an important supplement to the resources of poor families, but they, too, are far from adequate. Food stamps can be used in place of money to buy grocery items. The amount of food stamps a family can receive, however, is limited to approximately 50 cents per person per meal. Food stamps are not enough to keep children from being hungry and malnourished.

Why are so many American children homeless?

•The fastest growing group of homeless people in the nation are parents and their children. Some are young couples and their children like David and Sharla, whom you met at the beginning of this chapter.

•The loss of a job means inability to pay the rent or mortgage payment. For some families, the only solution is to move in with family or friends. Often, this results in situations where two or three families are living in a one-family home or apartment (Axelson & Dail, 1988, 467). Unlike David and Sharla, many young families may have no family or friends to whom they can turn. They and their children live in their car, a campground, or a makeshift shelter. Many of these families do not eat regularly. The children often do not go to school. They have almost nothing of their own, except worry, weariness, and growing hopelessness. Conservative estimates suggest that on any given night, there are 100,000 homeless children in the United States—more than all the children in Pittsburgh (CDF, 1991, 110).

•Children are homeless because poverty has deepened in our country, while housing costs have soared. Housing experts say that, generally, no more than one-third of a family's income should be spent on housing. Yet poor families with children are now paying an average of 70 to 75 percent of their income for housing (CDF, 1991, 111; Ziefert & Brown, 1991, 213). These families have little left to buy the other necessities of life—food, clothing, medical care. No matter how carefully they budget, an unexpected expense, or a dip in income, may find them unable to pay the rent, at risk of eviction and homelessness. The reasons for the housing crisis for poor families include deepening poverty in our nation, severe cuts in the government construction of low-cost housing, and the depletion of government loans for low-income housing development. Homeless families with children are the fastest growing group of homeless people in our nation (Guy, 1991, 85).

•**A large segment of homeless families are women escaping the abuse of their partners.** Trying to protect their children from family violence, they often have nowhere to turn. Many homeless families are refugees from family violence. Women have bundled up their children and fled from a partner who has physically hurt them or their children (Dail, 1990, 293).

What kinds of help are available for homeless families?

Homeless parents may be afraid to ask for help, fearful that having no home will be reason enough for a government agency to take their children away and place them in a children's emergency shelter or foster care. Other families find their way to homeless shelters. A few family shelters are places where these families can begin to put their lives back together. They provide the family with a safe place to stay for a short time while volunteer and professional staff help parents make plans and find resources.

Far more commonly, however, homeless shelters increase a family's stress, physical illness, sense of desperation, and numbing hopelessness. Many homeless shelters are barrack-style shelters with bunk beds or cots in large rooms shared by many families, or old single-room hotels. Families share bathrooms with everyone else in the shelter. Most shelters require that men and older boys be housed separately from women and younger children, making it hard for the family to hold together under overwhelming stress. Families may be allowed to cook in a common kitchen, or they may be served a daily meal or two. Children, who need more frequent and smaller meals, may often be hungry. There may be a television, but no safe place for the children to play, inside or outside. In such crowded, tiring conditions, diseases spread and children often become ill.

Shelters may be located in the most dangerous neighborhoods of a city. Some shelters are open only at night. Parents and children must spend the daytime hours on the city streets. The number of babies who die during the first year of life is 30 percent higher among homeless families (CDF, 1991, 108).

> Three-year-old Denise lived such a life. For a number of months she spent her nights with her mother, Barbara, and five-year-old brother, James, in a cubicle in a school gym that was used as a homeless shelter in Washington, D.C. Denise was awakened every morning at 5:30 when a staff member pounded on the side of their cubicle. At 7 A.M. a bus took Denise and her family across town to the welfare hotel where they waited for breakfast. After breakfast, the family boarded another bus to take James to a Head Start program. Most days, Denise was tired and cranky because the shelter closed during the day and there was no place for her to take the nap she needed. In the afternoon there was another bus ride to pick up James, dinner at the welfare hotel, and a final bus ride back to the gym (Guy, 1991, 86).

What impact does poverty and homelessness have on children?

• **Much of a poor parent's attention is focused on getting through each day and its crises**, which often center on food, shelter, safety in a dangerous community, and physical illness in a home which is drafty in winter and sweltering in summer. They must make do with faulty plumbing and heating. They find it difficult to provide their children with a protected, nurturing environment in which to grow, despite how much they love and provide for their children. Even if parents manage to keep their children adequately nourished, healthy, and feeling loved, children soon learn that they are not as valuable in our society because they are poor. In school, their backgrounds and life experiences may not compare positively with those of children who have attended preschool, traveled, and have parents with interesting careers. Poor children usually do not have encyclopedias in their homes, quiet places to study, or money for supplies for special projects or to participate in extracurricular school activities. Their parents usually do not have the kinds of jobs where they can take off in the middle of the day for a teacher conference or to accompany the class on a field trip.

•**Homeless children are at greater risk for emotional disturbance and school failure.** Homelessness traumatizes children. Homeless children have often moved a number of times, in and out of low-rent apartments or houses, to the homes of friends or family until they and their parents find themselves completely without shelter. With each move, children have lost something— familiar toys, clothing, and surroundings. Eventually, the family's belongings are limited to a few bags or boxes. Children may have had to change schools many times, or to miss many days of school. Many homeless children are afraid to go to school, afraid that their parents might have to move while they are in school and they will not be able to find them. It is hard for children to adjust to a new school and classmates, especially when they are embarrassed by the clothing they have to wear, or when they are hungry and tired from trying to sleep in a car or a noisy, unfamiliar shelter. Teachers report that homeless children often fall asleep at their desks. They often have poor health, or uncorrected vision or hearing problems, making it hard for them to do well in school. They have no quiet place to read or do homework. Imagine a child in a homeless family trying to prepare a project for a science fair. Half of homeless children over the age of five have symptoms of depression such as suicide attempts and high levels of anxiety. Their school performance is consistently below average, reflecting the chaos in their young lives (Dail, 1990, 293).

•Many homeless babies and preschoolers suffer from malnutrition, severe stomach disorders due to tainted formula, and poor weight gain and physical development. They also have higher rates of delayed social and emotional development than other children. The consequences of homelessness for children often last a lifetime.

Child Poverty in Your Community

Poverty wears different faces from community to community. The typical picture of poverty is often one of inner-city slums. But poor children live in suburbia and in rural areas, too. For example, well over 2,000 children are homeless in the rural counties of Kentucky (CDF, 1991, 111). The same is true in Iowa and Idaho and Arkansas—and probably in your state.

In learning what poverty looks like in your community, talk with people who work with poor children and their families. You may find the following people helpful in getting an overall picture of poverty in your community:

- a staff member from the local public assistance agency;
- a professional staff member from a community ministry agency in your neighborhood, or the person responsible for the use of benevolence funds in your congregation;
- a staff person of a sister church in your community which has programs serving poor children and families;
- the director of a shelter for homeless families;
- a staff member from the local housing authority;
- a representative from an advocacy group for poor and homeless families (look for a Habitat for Humanity chapter, Low-

Income Housing Coalition, or Coalition for the Homeless in your phone book);
• a teacher or school counselor from a school with large numbers of children living in poverty.

As you talk with the experts, find out what is required for a family to receive public assistance and food stamps, and how much assistance families normally receive. Ask them to help you develop a picture of the average budget for families receiving assistance in your community. Ask about the kinds of housing available for poor families. What poor families are not eligible for assistance? What other forms of aid are available? What kinds of help are churches in the community offering? What is being done to keep families from becoming homeless? What kind of shelter is available for homeless families, and how adequate is it?

When you have an overall picture of poverty in your community, put faces on the statistics and learn firsthand what poverty is like. Here are some ideas to guide you.
• Find the closest welfare office to your home. Wearing your less-than-best clothing, take whatever public transportation is available to that location. Ask to talk with a person who processes new applications for assistance. Learn what the requirements in your community are for economic assistance; you may want to propose a hypothetical situation, such as an abused spouse who feels she must leave home to protect herself and her children, but who has nowhere to go. Simply sit in the waiting room for a period of time, observing the people who come and go. Allow yourself to experience how it might feel if this were your only hope for finding a way to support your children.
• Visit the homeless shelter for families in your community or a shelter for victims of family violence, if there is one. If possible, have one or more of your group spend the night there and share their experiences with others in your church. Find out what services are available to families to help them cope with their cur-

rent crisis and make a better future for themselves.

• If there is no public shelter in your community, inquire with the police department about where homeless families usually find or make their own shelter, and what the police department's response is, if any.

• Lead your group through an imaginary experience. If this is done in a group, it may help to have people close their eyes in order to shut out distractions. Ask them to envision that they and/or their spouses have lost their jobs. They have spent all their savings just trying to survive these past months. Gradually, they have had to sell the furniture, the car, their other possessions in order to buy groceries and utilities. They no longer have money to pay the rent or mortgage, and they are losing their home. For whatever reasons, family cannot take them in. Where would they go? If you could only keep what you could carry yourself, what would you keep and what would you have to get rid of? What would it be like to sleep with your children on cots in a homeless shelter with other families, to have someone else decide when children should go to bed and get up, to eat all your meals in a cafeteria or soup kitchen and not to be able to decide what you or your children should eat, to have to carry all your possessions with you because the shelter closes during the day, and to be assigned a different space each night? What would worry you the most? Discuss this experience with one another.

• Drive or walk through one of the poorest neighborhoods in your community, preferably after school. Take companions with you for safety, if the area is one where crime is frequent. Note the adequacy of play areas for children. How would you feel if you were raising your children in this community? Visit a local grocery store in the community and compare prices with those in your neighborhood, remembering that poor families often do not have reliable automobiles which enable them to shop in the less expensive suburban supermarkets. Look for other community resources and needs.

• Using what you have learned about poverty in your community, imagine that you and/or your spouse have lost your job, and you must support two children on the average AFDC grant and food stamp allotment in your state for a family of four. Decide how you would budget your money for food, clothing, medical expenses, housing, and so on. Find out if there is public housing available in your community, and how long the waiting list is. Using the classified listings of last Sunday's paper, identify rental properties that would be within your financial reach. With one or more members of your congregation, ask to inspect apartments or houses. Share your experiences with your congregation.

• If your daily life does not bring you into relationship with poor children and families, find a way you can put faces and personal stories with the statistics of poverty in your community. Volunteer to work in an inner-city mission's after-school program, Vacation Bible School, or other programs for children and youth; offer to teach a craft class or another short-term course in a community center which serves poor families; volunteer to serve meals in a homeless shelter or soup kitchen. Allow poor families to teach you about poverty.

As you talk with caregivers in your community and develop relationships with poor children and their families, you form a picture of child poverty and homelessness in your own community. It can seem overwhelming, but there are ways you and your church can make a difference.

WHAT CHRISTIANS AND THEIR
CONGREGATIONS CAN DO

Individual Christians can take bold and effective action in response to the poverty of their neighbors. Church congregations can do even more. Here are suggestions and examples of what Christians and churches are doing.

Take your pastor and deacons on visits to social service agencies and poor neighborhoods. Include them in talking with experts whom you invite to speak to your church group. Invite them to join the discussion of what you have learned, of God's purposes for the church in ministry, and of how your congregation might respond to the needs you have seen. Encourage your pastor to preach a sermon series on the needs of poor children and families, urging your congregation to take concrete action.

As a consequence of their mission outreach with families in the community, the pastor and deacons of The First Baptist Church of Rosedale became increasingly concerned about the high rate of unemployment among older teens and young adults. Many preschool and young school-age children were growing up in poverty because their parents could not find work. Several business people in the church organized a mission action group. First they studied the issues of unemployment and poverty in their community. They then organized a program they called JOBS, offering training in job interview skills, providing a computer and guidance in developing resumes, and offering support and advice to young adults looking for employment. They also developed an informal network of public and private opportunities and programs for job training, and a scholarship fund to help those who wanted to continue their education. Free child care was provided for parents participating in the JOBS course, and scholarships were available for the children of participants for the church's day-care and after-school-care programs while parents attended school or looked for work.

Others in the church organized a work crew and, with the help of neighborhood residents and the support of city government, cleaned up and built a playground in a park in a low-income area which had become a dumping ground for trash. The playground became a place for young parents to meet and talk together in the afternoons while children played. A neighborhood meeting was called by the church, inviting community residents to come and talk over their concerns. As a consequence, a neighborhood watch program was organized and another community meeting with police was planned to discuss parents' concerns for children's safety in the community. Police presence in the community was increased, and the neighborhood began to develop a sense of community identity and pride.

Create or support a fund in your church which provides loans and aid to families who need assistance. Many churches have emergency funds to help families. If you do not have such a ministry in your congregation, consider beginning one. Assistance in paying a utility bill, a security deposit, or a rent down payment may prevent a poor family from loss of utilities or homelessness. Church secretaries and other staff often are not able to give the time and care which families need when they call asking for help. Perhaps volunteers in the congregation could respond to such calls. Some churches have a simple shoebox file with cards. They enter the names of families they have helped, along with the date and kind of help provided. Other churches have computer data bases which relate to other churches and community agencies, in an attempt to provide help to the families who need it most without duplicating the efforts of others. Talk with other churches in your community and the staff of community agencies who work with poor families so that you can develop a system which fits your resources and the needs of poor families in your community.

Participate in community ministries. In some communities, churches organize and coordinate their efforts so as to be more effective in provision of emergency assistance to families. Some have developed neighborhood agencies called "community ministries" through which they channel ministry. These agencies may operate out of several of the church buildings in the community. A day-care center may be located in one church, a Mother's Day Out program for children with needs in another church, and emergency assistance and a jobs resource program in yet another church. The community ministries agency tries to develop whatever programs will best serve the needs of the community, including day care for children, after-school care, family crisis counseling, support groups for recovering alcoholics or persons with other special needs, a play group for preschoolers, emergency assistance (food, clothing, money for rent and utilities), transportation for the elderly or for young parents and children with health needs, family life education programs, and even emergency shelter.

Community ministries are able to capture a broad picture of the needs and coordinate the ministries of several congregations with more impact than one congregation working on its own. In addition, they speak with a loud voice and can advocate for change in some of the factors which create poverty in families.

Churches in Louisville, Kentucky, cooperate with one another by financially supporting an extensive network of community ministries. Much of the emergency assistance for families is available through these ministries. A few years ago, the volunteers and staff who work in these agencies discovered that most of their financial assistance was going to pay high utility bills of poor families, particularly during cold winters. They developed a winterization program that organized volunteers to make home repairs and install insulation in the homes of poor families who were paying too much of their income for utilities. In addition, they organized churches and community residents to bring pressure to bear on the utility company to develop a more equitable rate system for poor families.

Volunteer to work in a shelter for homeless families or other programs which serve the poor in your community. Many homeless shelters depend on volunteers. You may be asked to serve meals or meet new families who are asking for shelter. Or you may provide friendship and support to families, help them to celebrate birthdays or other special events, and work with them in developing and implementing a plan for putting their lives back together. The professional staff of shelters should provide training and support for your work.

Churches located in or near areas of low-income housing often have developed extensive service programs including activity and recreation programs for children and youth, adult education courses for parents, and programs which attend to the special needs of families. Often churches who are not so located encourage their members and missions groups to offer their services to sister churches and missions. If your church participates in a community ministry as described above, it will also encourage your volunteer service through that ministry.

Paul and Susan felt compelled to find some way to develop a bridge between their affluent suburban congregation and a poor community a few miles away in another part of the city. They volunteered their services to a small congregation which was trying to develop an outreach program for community families. Paul and Susan began by leading a children's Bible study and activity group on Wednesday night. They wanted to learn about the community through the eyes of its children. Through the group, Paul and Susan became particularly attached to a young brother and sister, Tyrone and Shawna, who attended faithfully. Over the months that followed, Paul and Susan visited in Tyrone's and Shawna's home and developed a friendship with the children's mother, Brenda, a young single mother attending the community college's nursing degree program. Her goal was to find employment as a nurse and free her family from dependence on a meager AFDC grant. At times, Paul and Susan were able to help with a gift for the children of a needed article of clothing, an outing for the children while Brenda studied, and always with their encouragement and sympathetic support. A highlight of their relationship was taking Brenda and the children on a weekend camping trip. The relationship has become a special and mutual friendship, something Paul and Susan had not counted on when they began their work with the children's Bible study two years ago.

Offer a poor or homeless family ongoing assistance and support. Assist the family with its basic needs, such as housing, food, and a job. Include the family in your church. Like Brenda and her children, some families appreciate having a friend who cares. They may also need help finding a job, a place to live, furniture, or clothing. Your pastor, a community ministries agency, or a public social service agency can put you in touch with a family who needs your care. If you make a contact through an agency, be sure to talk with a professional staff member about your desire to be helpful in a personal way with a specific family. He or she will be able to help you think through ways you can help and be sensitive to the family's needs without embarrassing them.

Find ways to use the church's existing programs to provide support and assistance to poor and homeless families. Find ways to reach out to poor and homeless families, including their children in your church's day-care center, after-school activity programs, Sunday School, family recreation evenings, or other ministries. Poor families are often dependent on public transportation, making it difficult for them to participate. Offer to provide transportation to make their participation possible.

Contribute money, materials and/or your own work to build suitable housing for low-income families. Many congregations have joined with groups such as Habitat for Humanity or other nonprofit organizations to build or rehabilitate low-cost housing. Habitat for Humanity builds affordable low-cost housing that poor families can purchase for far less than they would pay for rent. The homes are built by volunteers, with the families themselves contributing some of the labor. The money families pay for their new homes is used to build other homes for other families. You and your congregation can actually be the developer and builder, or can provide financial resources or workers. For help, contact Habitat for Humanity International (121 Habitat Street, Americus, GA 31709, 912-924-6935).

Make your voice heard in favor of government programs to increase the supply of low-cost housing and the provision of income support programs for families in economic crisis. Emergency help is necessary, but it will not solve the root problems of poverty. Although the church is called to feed the hungry and shelter the homeless, often the damage to children's lives has already been done before we reach them with our ministry efforts, damage done by the chronic anxiety and upheaval they have experienced because their family is poor. Churches cannot single-handedly do away with poverty and homelessness. We can make our voices heard, however, for a more just society. Local, state, and federal government representatives need to hear that their constituency, the people in the churches in the communities they serve, want them to make housing assistance available to poor families and to raise AFDC benefits and minimum wages to levels at which low-income families can afford to meet the basic needs of their children.

SEEKING JUSTICE, LOVING KINDNESS, WALKING HUMBLY WITH GOD

In a nation as wealthy as ours, all children should have adequate food, necessary clothing, a safe home, needed medical care, and the security that parents will be able to meet these basic needs into the future. We consider David's and Sharla's children the lucky ones; at least they had grandparents to whom they could turn. Yet the self-esteem of their parents is being destroyed because they cannot meet the basic needs of their children. Their marriage is in crisis because they have neither privacy for working through their difficulties, nor opportunity for the intimacy which nourishes a marriage, nor hope for making things better. Their children suffer from parents too depressed and frightened to be able to help their children with their insecurities, too numbed by day after day of crisis to help their children grow with hope and promise.

Praise the Lord.
Praise the Lord, O my soul.
I will praise the Lord all my life;
I will sing praise to my God as long as I live.

Do not put your trust in princes,
in mortal men, who cannot save.
When their spirit departs, they return to the ground;
on that very day their plans come to nothing.

Blessed is he whose help is the God of Jacob,
whose hope is in the Lord his God,
the Maker of heaven and earth,
the sea, and everything in them—
the Lord, who remains faithful forever.
He upholds the cause of the oppressed
and gives food to the hungry (Psalm 146:1-7 NIV).

Psalm 146 sings out that God is both Creator of the universe and defender of the poor. Bringing justice for the poor and hungry is just as essential a characteristic of God as bringing the very heavens and earth into existence (Sider, 1977). God cares for poor and hungry children because of who God is. We seek justice for poor and hungry children because we belong to this God of justice and love.

Seeking justice means speaking out to our communities and to our government officials on behalf of the poor. As necessary as they are, shelters for the homeless and remedial services for poor children are not enough; they point to our failures as a nation, not to our compassion. Homelessness and the crippling effects of poverty can be prevented by government policies which ensure an adequate income for families, which encourage and directly support the development of low-income housing. It is "seeking justice" to let our voices be heard in support of programs of economic support for families.

Poverty and homelessness cripple the spirits of children and families. Even if these blights on our society were eliminated today, we would still need to care for those whose self-esteem and competencies have dwindled by their effects. As long as poverty and homelessness are with us, we are called to minister to the poor and the homeless. It is "loving kindness" to care enough to offer friendship to a poor child, to reach out with sensitive care and support to a family during hard times, to prepare and serve meals in a soup kitchen, or drive a poor mother and her sick child to visit the doctor.

In response to the disciples' indignation over a woman wasting expensive ointment on Jesus which could have been sold to feed the poor, Jesus said that the poor would always be with us, although "you will not always have me" (Matt. 26:11). The problem of poverty is ancient; few of us expect it to be eliminated in our lifetime. Yet Jesus was not saying to give up. In fact, He had just told the disciples to feed the hungry and give drink to the thirsty (Matt. 25). He challenged them to ministry, because to minister to the "least of these" was a direct way of caring for the Lord. Through the experience of being served so lavishly by the woman with her ointment, He again made the context of our ministry clear. There is a reality which is bigger than poverty, and that is Jesus' presence with us and our call to serve Him. When Christians feed the hungry, we do so as a way of caring for our Lord. We cannot serve our Lord in human flesh as the woman did with her ointment, but we can serve our Lord in the human flesh of the poor; they are Jesus in our midst. In humility, we recognize that our call for justice and our loving kindness are offered not with the end goal of eliminating all poverty. If that is our goal, we will fail. Instead, they are the ways we can serve Jesus, ways we can walk humbly with our God.

"He who is kind to the poor lends to the Lord,
and he will reward him for what he has done"
(Prov. 19:17 NIV).

"He who oppresses the poor shows contempt for their Maker,
but whoever is kind to the needy honors God"
(Prov. 14:31 NIV).

Resources

Axelson, Leland J., and Dail, Paula W. 1988. "The Changing Character of Homelessness in the United States." *Family Relations, 37*, 463-469.
A fascinating review of the history of homelessness in the United States and an overview of contemporary homelessness. The authors examine the current housing crisis, the social impact of homelessness, the nature of shelter services, and public policy concerns.

Bailey, Patricia L. 1992. "Social Work Practice in Community Ministries." In Diana R. Garland (Ed.) *Church Social Work*. St. Davids, PA: The North American Association of Christians in Social Work, pp. 58-65.
Describes community ministries, which are organizations of churches of different denominations within a community to respond to the human needs of neighbors. Addresses the issues which need to be considered in developing such a ministry in one's own community.

Barrett, John M. 1988. *It's Hard Not To Worry: Stories for Children About Poverty*. New York: Friendship Press.
Stories for school-age children about children whose families face unemployment, farm foreclosure, and other forms of poverty in America. Stories conclude with discussion questions for families or children's groups.

Bos, David. 1985. "Community Ministries: The Establishment of Ecumenical Local Mission North American Church Life." *Journal of Ecumenical Studies, 22* (1), 121-127.
An overview of the development of community ministries and practical considerations in developing these programs.

Edelman, Marian Wright. 1987. *Families in Peril: An Agenda for Social Change*. Cambridge: Harvard University Press.
Describes the overall status of black and white children and families in America, the human and financial costs of our widespread child and family poverty, and how we are failing our children.

Parham, Robert. 1988. *What Shall We Do in a Hungry World?* Birmingham: New Hope.
Provides a moving overview of the presence of hunger in our world and our own nation, and describes what Southern Baptists are doing in response.

Schorr, Lisbeth B. 1988. *Within Our Reach: Breaking the Cycle of Disadvantage.* New York: Anchor Press.

A review of the factors that create "rotten outcomes" for children and youth— teenaged pregnancy, leaving school illiterate and unemployable, and committing violent crimes. Schorr looks at programs which are working successfully in the area of teen pregnancy, prenatal care, child health services, education, and poverty.

Sider, Ronald. 1980. *Cry Justice: The Bible on Hunger and Poverty.* Downers Grove, IL: InterVarsity Press.

A collection of Biblical texts designed to assist in the careful study of the Bible's teachings on poverty, possessions, justice, faithful stewardship, and costly discipleship.

Sider, Ronald. 1977. *Rich Christians in An Age of Hunger.* Downers Grove, IL: InterVarsity Press.

Provides a Biblical perspective on poverty, hunger, property, and wealth. Suggests practical proposals for individual Christians and church communities who want to live more simply and actively care for the world's poor and hungry.

5

Children Without Hope

ONE CHILD'S STORY

In chapter 1, you met Darlene, the homeless teenaged mother of two-year-old Robert. A school dropout, she had no hopeful prospects for herself or her son, no income, no home, no job. That was two years ago, but Darlene's story has a happy ending—or beginning. While living in the shelter for homeless families, Darlene met Katherine, a member of a missions group from a Baptist church working with the shelter. A social worker on the staff of the shelter pairs each volunteer from the church with a mother living in the shelter. Katherine is a mother of young children herself, though ten years older than Darlene. She knows how demanding a two-year-old can be. While the social worker helped Darlene find a modest apartment and apply for an AFDC grant, Katherine provided friendship and encouragement. Katherine and Darlene drank coffee together, laughed and cried together, talked about mothering, and discussed the decisions facing Darlene. With Katherine's encouragement, Darlene began to believe that she might be able to go back to school and become a nurse, something she dreamed about as a small child. At first, Katherine went with Darlene to a class which enabled her to receive her high school equivalency certificate.

Katherine also invited Darlene to the Young Mothers Group offered by the church. Mothers can continue to participate in the Young Mothers Group after they have moved to their own housing. The church picks up the mothers, since transportation is hard for them. It also provides free child care while the group meets. The group has a dual focus. First, it encourages women to see their potential and to take charge of their futures. Second, the program focuses on teaching them about child development and the skills of parenting. There is time just to talk, however, and there is always a lot of laughter and fun. The group often plans outings that include the children.

Through Katherine's friendship and the Young Mothers Group, Darlene has begun to believe that she can make something of her life. She received her high school equivalency certificate and is planning to go to college to study nursing next fall, although it will be difficult to go to school and care for her young son. Katherine is helping her find out about financial assistance while she is in school. Whatever happens, Darlene does not have to face it alone. Katherine and the other women in the church and the Young Mothers Group will make sure of that.

Other stories do not have such happy endings. Not every teen parent finds a Christian friend who can help her over the rough spots and into a future that looks brighter. Many high school dropouts do not go back to school. They end up with futures very different than what we want for them. We want all children to be well-educated, to have jobs they find satisfying and with incomes that will support themselves and a family.

THE FACTS ABOUT SCHOOL FAILURE, SUBSTANCE ABUSE, AND TEEN PREGNANCY

School failure, substance abuse, and early pregnancy are symptoms that tell us that we are falling short of giving children hopeful futures. These problems keep teens from moving into healthy, productive adulthood. School failure, substance abuse, and teen pregnancy also cause less than hopeful futures for the children of teen parents. Pregnant teenagers often receive inadequate or no prenatal care, meaning that their babies are at increased risk of being born at low birth weight. Low birth weight is associated with a number of serious physical and mental handicaps including learning disabilities. Teen parents are often poor, meaning that their children are less likely to receive adequate nutrition and good medical care.

Poor parents have difficulty providing safe, stimulating homes and child care in which children can grow. Children who are ill, undernourished, or undernurtured are less likely to do well in school. One research study reported that 50 percent of the children of teen mothers had repeated one grade, 17 percent were in remedial classes, and nearly 50 percent had serious behavior problems in school (Ooms, 1989, ii). And so the cycle repeats itself; the children of teen parents are likely to do poorly in school, to use drugs, to become teen parents.

The seeds of school failure, substance abuse, and teen pregnancy are sown in the preschool and early school-age years. Adolescents who drop out of school, who become involved in delinquency, and who become teenaged parents have children who show problems with school, especially in reading, as early as the third grade (Schorr, 1988, 14, 221). Disadvantaged children often are not ready for first grade. Head Start, a highly successful program that prepares disadvantaged children for school, has never been fully funded and currently reaches only 25 percent of eligible children, although funding has been increased for the future (Guy, 1991, 67). By the third grade, some children have fallen far behind, and those behind in reading will tend to fall further and further behind. They not only have difficulty in reading, but they have difficulty in all the other subjects that depend on reading. Early on, children form opinions of themselves. Children with low self-esteem expect to fail; they stop trying. It becomes difficult to persuade them that school is important.

Many adolescents are leaving school ill-prepared for adult life and unemployable. In 1900, 90 percent of youngsters did not graduate from high school, but it was not a problem. In the 1950s, when half dropped out before graduation, it was still not much of a concern because there were many jobs young adult could find that did not require a high school education. They could still support themselves and their young families. All that has changed with the technological developments of the past 25 years. Now there is only one way children can succeed in the adult world of employment—education. Yet, almost 29 percent of American young people who entered the ninth grade in 1984 failed to graduate from high school four years later (CDF, 1991, 76). Even those who remain in school may fail to be educated.

• Among 17-year-olds who are still in school, only half can compute using decimals, fractions, and percents; fewer than half can understand, summarize, and explain the kind of material found in encyclopedias or high school texts.

• Among 13-year-olds, 27 percent cannot add, subtract, multiply, and divide using whole numbers; and 42 percent cannot search for specific information, interrelate ideas, and make generalizations about something they have just read (CDF, 1991, p. 76-77).

Even young people who stay in school may graduate unable to follow an instruction form, fill out a job application, read a newspaper, or develop and follow a budget. Those with weak reading and math skills are four times more likely to become dependent on welfare as adults than those with strong skills. They are eight times more likely to become single parents (Schorr, 1988, 10).

Although use of illicit drugs is declining among children and youth, alcohol use is a widespread threat to teenagers' healthy development. For the past five to ten years, use of illicit drugs among teens has been declining, although it still threatens to engulf the futures of some of our children. In a 1989 survey, 17 percent of high school seniors reported using marijuana in the previous month; 3 percent had used it daily. Of course, young people who have dropped out of school may use drugs at a much higher rate. Alcohol remains a widespread threat to teenagers' current health and safety as well as their futures as productive adults. In a 1989 survey, one-third of high school seniors reported that they had engaged in heavy drinking (five drinks or more in a row) during the past two weeks (CDF, 1991, 97).

One out of every four babies in the United States is born to a single mother. Each year, 1 million American teenaged girls become pregnant; on an average, one out of three girls is pregnant before she reaches age 20 (Family Impact Seminar, 1990, 1). One out of five girls is sexually active by age 15, and the average age at which all girls become sexually active is now 16, long before marriage. By age 15, 27 percent of girls and 33 percent of boys have engaged in sexual intercourse; by age 17, 50 percent of girls and 66 percent of boys have had intercourse (CDF, 1991, 93). Typically, teenagers wait a year after engaging in intercourse the first time before they begin to use contraception, often too late to prevent pregnancy.

Only 4 percent of pregnant teens choose adoption as a response to pregnancy; 40 percent of teenaged pregnancies end in abortion; 13 percent end with a miscarriage (a higher rate than adults since a teenager's body is often not mature enough to carry a pregnancy to term), and almost half choose to parent their babies (Adams, Adams-Taylor, & Pittman, 1989, 224). Teenaged girls who become pregnant experience dramatic changes in their physical and emotional health, regardless of the outcome of the pregnancy. Those who choose to parent babies face diminished life choices.

Church members sometimes respond to statistics with remarks such as, "But I was a teenager when I had my first child; what's wrong with that?" Indeed, today's middle-aged mothers and grandmothers often had their first babies when they were teenagers, but they were usually older teens—and they were married. In 1960, only 16 percent of births occurred outside of marriage. Today's teens who give birth are more likely to be single than married; 61 percent of teenaged mothers are not married at the time of delivery. In 1970, one baby in nine was born to a single mother; in 1988, one baby out of four was born to a single mother. Most teenagers who do marry will experience divorce, suggesting that teenaged marriage is only a temporary cure for single parenthood. Teenaged mothers are most likely to be poor, not only as teenagers, but for the rest of their lives. They earn an average of half the lifetime income of women who wait until age 20 or longer to have their first baby. Their babies, therefore, will probably grow up poor, in single-parent or blended families (Edelman, 1987, 56).

Multiple factors put teens at risk for a pregnancy outside of marriage.

1. **Ignorance**. Teens often have wrong or inadequate information. Although they may have participated in a sex education course in school, they may have been too embarrassed to seek answers to their questions. They often learn about sex and sexuality from friends who are inadequately informed themselves. Teenagers learn by talking things over; talking with parents or peers has more meaning than watching a film or reading a book.

2. **Sense of invincibility**. Teens are notorious for their belief that "it won't happen to me." They are heady with a growing sense of identity and autonomy and find it difficult to believe that bad things can happen to them. They are learning about the world and themselves by experimentation, testing their limits. For many, this means driving too fast and trying new experiences including drugs, alcohol, and sex.

3. **Strength of sexual feelings**. Emotionally, interpersonally, spiritually, and practically, teens are not usually ready for the responsibility which comes with sexual intimacy, although they are physically mature. Teens have strong physical drives that demand to be recognized and require mature self-understanding and self-responsibility to channel appropriately.

4. **Peer group pressure**. Teens are attuned keenly to the nuances of their peer group's expectations. The peer group provides the most significant mirror in which teens can check out, affirm, or alter their growing, but still quite vulnerable, sense of self. The peer group can make all the difference to the teen in its support either for setting appropriate boundaries or for sexual experimentation and exploitation.

5. **Poor self-esteem**. Teens with low self-esteem are especially at risk for pregnancy. The affirmation of one's attractiveness and the special affection identified with sexual intimacy appeal to teens who do not believe that others find them attractive or special. Teens who are doing poorly in school may yearn for the feeling of achievement which may be provided by winning the focus of someone else's attention or by persuading a partner to engage in sexual intercourse. Teens with low self-esteem who are doing poorly in school are almost six times more likely to experience pregnancy than teens in general (Edelman, 1987, 55). Carrying a baby may be the only thing a teenaged girl thinks she can do that is special. A teenaged boy may think that the best way he can "score" in life is by sexual activity and impregnating a girlfriend.

6. **Pressure from a partner**. A boyfriend's or girlfriend's continuing love and commitment can be all-important to the teenager. Consequently, the pressure of "If you loved me, you would . . ." is especially difficult to resist for a teen who has not experienced much love and affection in other important relationships. Both boys and girls pressure their partners to have sexual intercourse, and boys may find it especially difficult to resist a girlfriend's insistence, since our culture implies that to reject her request for sexual intimacy calls his virility into question.

7. **Use of alcohol and drugs**. Alcohol and other drugs serve to lower inhibitions and reasoning capabilities. Teens often experiment with substances without adult supervision, thus inhibiting the normal safeguards for their behavior. They find themselves pushed into decisions made impulsively with clouded minds.

8. **Media**. Television, movies, and popular music bombard teens with the message that "everyone is doing it." Our culture's efforts to curb the AIDS epidemic by promoting "safe sex" have made the choices even more confusing. The message seems to be that sex is permissible as long as one is "safe," which means taking precautions to avoid disease and pregnancy. Christian parents also may be confused by the media, wondering if their belief that sex should be saved for marriage is so outdated as to be irrelevant for helping their children make the choices which face them. They want to protect their children from disease and too-early pregnancy, but they fear that teens will misconstrue any talk about "safe sex" as indirect permission to engage in sexual activity. As a consequence, teens get mixed messages from their parents—or no messages at all. They are left with the ever-present message of the media.

9. **Lack of responsibility for their behavior**. Teens often have difficulty taking responsibility for what they have done or might do. Many assume that accidents just happen, and no one has to feel responsible. As a consequence, they may ignore the possible repercussions of their behavior, perhaps saying to themselves: *It just happened, and I won't let it happen again.* They may refuse to recognize that their behavior places them in situations where they can allow their feelings and those of their partner to lead them into sexual intimacy. To allow themselves to recognize and plan what they are doing, which is necessary if they are to use some form of contraception, seems more sinful than allowing an accident to happen. This attitude makes

the use of birth control measures virtually impossible and accounts for sexually active teens delaying an average of one year between first intercourse and first use of an effective method of birth control.

10. **Troubled family relationships.** Teens who are embarrassed to talk with their parents or fearful of their parents' response cannot get needed support from them and, therefore, may rely on peers. If teens feel unloved by parents, they may seek needed love from a boyfriend or girlfriend, and perhaps even from a baby. Pregnancy does elevate the status of the young mother, who is accorded with more respect and treated less like a girl and more like a woman.

Many teens may have troubled relationships with their parents or may be especially sensitive to peer pressure, yet they do not experience a too-early pregnancy. As the number of factors in the list above increases in the life of a teenager, however, the risk of pregnancy also increases. Therefore, pregnancy prevention involves more than simply educating teens about sex. As important and needed as sex education courses are in school, such courses alone cannot effectively confront this complexity of factors. Ignorance of the facts of life is only one of many risk factors, and perhaps the easiest to correct. A comprehensive response is needed. Churches can respond directly to the needs of adolescents; churches can empower parents to tackle the forces in the lives of their children which place them at risk. Christians can advocate for changes in communities and schools which will give all teens viable life choices that are preferable to teenaged parenting.

Hope for the future is the best prevention of school failure, substance abuse, and teen pregnancy. The best contraception and drug prevention program for teens is hope for a future that will meet their needs, challenge their capacities, and give their lives purpose and meaning. A hopeful future makes waiting for sexual intimacy seem worthwhile, the escape through drugs unnecessary. Any effort to reduce teen pregnancy must focus on promoting school success. Girls who become pregnant as teens usually have a history of school problems and failures. They see little possibility of a decent job or economic independence for themselves. Sex and pregnancy are their routes to adulthood. Similarly, 18- and 19-year-old boys with poor school performances are three times as likely to be fathers as those who have done average or better in school (Schorr, 1988, 62).

Sex education programs alone will not prevent teen pregnancy (Christopher & Roosa, 1990, 68-72). Pregnancy prevention requires knowledge about sexuality, but it also requires the ability to discipline one's self and to make hard choices and stick to them. Many factors contribute to self-discipline. The discipline and self-esteem that come from playing team sports, taking music lessons, and feeling competent in school all contribute directly to self-esteem and self-control and thus, indirectly, to wise decisions about sexuality and subsequent behavior. Teens need not only to learn to say *no*; they need to say *yes* to future goals and dreams and to the importance of commitment and responsibility in relationships. Disadvantaged teens, in particular, need compelling reasons not to get pregnant, compelling goals to which they can say *yes*. They need life options created by education that offer hope for a future not shackled by poverty.

We need also to recognize that "earlier help would have been better help" (Schorr, 1988, p. xxvii). The factors which lead to school failure and teen pregnancy are in place long before the teenage years. Older elementary and middle school-age children (ages 10 to 13) are a particularly vulnerable group. For many disadvantaged children and youth, decisions or non-decisions will be made during these years that irrevocably shape their futures. Special attention needs to be given to ensure that preteens, as well as teenagers, have:

- nurturing families that provide security, discipline, and love;
- good schools that encourage achievement of all students, including those who are disadvantaged;
- caring relationships with adults who serve as positive role models and friends;
- recreational programs and activities that build confidence and self-esteem and encourage positive peer group relationships;
- opportunities to make contributions to the lives of others and develop skills needed in the workplace and in community life;
- a safe place where adults and peers help them explore concerns and where they can be encouraged and empowered to take responsibility for their behavior; and
- sex education programs which emphasize the value of saving sex for marriage but are also sensitive to the fact that some teens will choose to engage in sexual intercourse.

In addition, many preteens and teens need sex education that is sensitive to the fact that they have been sexually abused. A program which focuses exclusively on saving sex for marriage may compound their hurt by implicitly labeling them as damaged or no longer virgin because of their nonvoluntary sexual experience. Because these teens often have low self-esteem and an altered sense of self, they are particularly vulnerable to teen pregnancy. In one study, 54 percent of teen mothers reported that they had been sexually abused by the age of 18 (Butler & Burton, 1990, 73).

Some teens choose to be sexually active. Though we may not agree with their choice, they still need adults to encourage them to take responsibility for their behavior by protecting themselves and others from sexually transmitted diseases and pregnancy.

Caring about young people means seeing that their needs are met. As you begin to talk with teenagers in your own church and community and to study the schools, supplementary educational programs, and other community programs designed for teenagers, think about them from the perspective of the list of needs above.

TEENS IN YOUR COMMUNITY

There are a number of resources for learning about the extent of problems with school failure, teenaged pregnancy, and teen substance abuse in your community. You will also want to find out what your community is doing in response to these problems. You may find numerous programs designed to encourage disadvantaged youth to succeed in school; to prevent early pregnancy and provide crisis pregnancy services; to prevent substance abuse and help teens involved with drugs; and to help teen parents survive. The following people can help you study the problems and responses in your community:

- youth ministers in your church and in other neighborhoods of your town or city;
- local school board members;
- counselors in the middle schools and high schools, and in teen parenting educational programs;
- staff members of social service agencies which serve teens;
- social workers from the staff of your denominational agency which serves children and youth and their families; and
- literature from the Children's Defense Fund.

As you learn about programs which serve your community's youth, look for signs of effectiveness in addressing the problems of school failure, substance abuse, and teen pregnancy. Be alert to the needs of preteens and seek ways your church might be able to help. The Children's Defense Fund suggests that good programs:

- have several ways for teens to become involved: remedial services (tutoring, counseling), crisis intervention, and enrichment activities (recreation and youth organizations);
- offer year-round programs that are open long hours—evenings and weekends;
- attract a wide age group, allowing youth to interact with people of various ages;

- provide ongoing support and do not require youth to stop participating at a certain age or after a certain time period;
- have the capacity to reach out to youth in the community and to coordinate services with other helping professionals for the best interest of a particular teen being served; and
- refer them to other community services they need and advocate in their behalf (CDF, 1991, 102).

WHAT CHURCH GROUPS AND CONGREGATIONS CAN DO

Church programs for youth provide hope and encouragement, positive peer group and self-esteem-enhancing activities, and relationships with caring adults that have made all the difference for generations of teenagers. The children's and youth ministries of churches continue to play an essential role in the lives of many young people. In addition, there are some particular ways churches can supplement their youth ministries to reach disadvantaged youth and those at risk for substance abuse, school failure, and early pregnancy.

Provide tutoring and educational support for disadvantaged children. Patterns of educational success and failure are established in the elementary school years. Programs which can help disadvantaged children succeed in school in the early years help prevent school failure, substance abuse, and pregnancy in the teenaged years.

Christ United Methodist Church adopted Henderson Elementary School in Baltimore, Maryland. On Monday, church women have breakfast with disadvantaged children who participate in the federally funded breakfast program. The women informally chat with children about events in their lives at home and school. The women developed a creative dance program that has attracted both boys and girls, a Reading Partners project to help children with reading difficulties, and a neighborhood cleanup project for the whole community on Saturdays. They provide special field trips once a month to reward students for good behavior in the classroom. When a child has problems, a teacher may call the child's volunteer reading partner and ask her to come to school. The volunteer sits with the child in the classroom and helps the child concentrate on schoolwork. After school, the two of them work on the problem. The program is reducing the number of expulsions and keeping children from falling behind academically. It also helps the church identify families that need further assistance (Guy, 1991, 126).

Offer programs which teach knowledge and values about sexuality. Provide opportunities to develop skills which enable teens to make wise choices about sexuality, drugs, and their futures. These programs can be part of regular youth activities. It is wise to let parents know what you are planning and encourage their input, since parents are concerned about what their children are taught about sex and sexuality at church or at school. Care needs to be taken that parents do not view sex education programs as usurpers of their responsibility as parents. Programming should include parents and give them a major role in the planning and implementation of sex education and pregnancy prevention programs. Research indicates that daughters whose mothers have talked with them about their sexuality are less likely to become pregnant as teens than girls whose mothers have not talked with them (Ooms, 1981, 98). One could surmise that the sexual behavior of boys is similarly related to their relationships with their parents.

Some churches offer seminars and discussion groups for parents of teens and include the topics of sexuality, teen pregnancy, and substance abuse. Guides for parents and programs on sex and sexuality are available for all ages from the Sunday School Board of the Southern Baptist Convention; some of these are listed at the end of this chapter. It is particularly critical that we offer guidance and support to preteens in these areas of decision-making.

> The Presbyterian Church of the Palms in Sarasota, Florida, developed a 12-week course, Boys and Babies, for 12-year-old boys. Parents who have infants in the church's child-care center gave permission for their babies to be diapered, fed, and played with by the boys in the class. The program teaches boys to care enough about babies that they will not help create one before they are ready to be good fathers. The program includes content about sexuality and films on the growth of a baby before it is born (Guy, 1991, 129).

Provide communication workshops for parents and their children. Any program which strengthens relationships between parents and teens contributes to teenage pregnancy prevention. Young people with strong, healthy relationships with their parents are much more likely to choose to delay sexual activity until they are older (Ooms, 1981, 93) and to say no to drugs. The most direct route to strengthening relationships may be teen/parent programs which teach parents and teens how to talk and listen to one another, how to reach decisions and compromise with one another, and how to understand one another's different world views. Such programs can combine sessions for teen and parent groups with sessions for teens and parents together. There are many program resources, some of which you will find listed at the end of this chapter.

Programs with other overt goals may also have the implicit objectives of strengthening parent-teen relationships. Church family camping and retreats, missions projects, and many other programs can include within them elements of meaningful parent-teen interaction.

Include content on sexuality in other programs of the church, including sermons and Bible study. Our sexuality is a gift of God; the intimacy of the relationship between a man and a woman reflects the very nature of God. We share in God's creative activity in bringing forth new life from our union with one another through pregnancy, birth, and parenting. Our sexuality is an integral part of our spiritual nature. Teens who are making decisions about their relationships with the opposite sex and the use of their bodies are making spiritual decisions. Teens who are sexually active or who have been victims of sexual abuse need to hear clearly the message of God's grace and love, and to be helped in claiming the new creation we are promised as Christians. They need to feel the support of a Christian community. Pregnancy prevention and sex education, therefore, belong at the heart of a church's youth and family ministries and need to be rooted in our theology and faith, and in our life together as people of God.

Organize teen tutoring and recreational programs and seek out disadvantaged youth, those who are at risk for school failure, substance abuse, and teenaged pregnancy. In many respects, all youth activities which build a cohesive, positive peer group in a church community can be considered pregnancy prevention. When teenagers are involved in church recreation and missions activities, they are being supervised by adults and simply have less time to get into trouble. When programming is designed to teach cooperation rather than competition and to encourage teens to support and befriend one another, they are building one another's self-esteem and, paradoxically, the ability to withstand peer pressure. When teens are encouraged to discuss the hard questions with one another, they can substitute the fantasy world of the media and its pressures with the real experiences of listening to peers who share their values and dilemmas.

Operation Getting It Together (OGIT) serves low-income and minority persons in Sonoma County, California. It is sponsored by 14 local churches representing seven denominations, including two Southern Baptist churches. The Youth Outreach Program of OGIT carefully screens, trains, and supervises high school juniors, seniors, and college students, called youth outreach workers, who are teamed with no more than two children living in poverty who are considered at risk for school failure and/or delinquency. Outreach workers provide friendship, guidance, positive role modeling, help with school, and sharing of worthwhile experiences in the larger geographical area. The outreach workers must submit brief written monthly progress reports, attend quarterly training workshops, and commit themselves to at least five hours per week with their assigned youngster for a minimum of one year. They receive a modest monthly expense allowance to pay for activities and transportation, and a $300 annual community service scholarship; some receive school credit for their involvement in the program.

Some years ago, the principal of a local elementary school referred Paul to Operation Getting It Together (OGIT). Paul was in the sixth grade and was having problems in school, the community, and at home. According to the principal, Paul had three difficulties: He was a born leader, but he was leading all the other students in the wrong direction; he was a natural athlete, but he refused to become involved in any of the school's athletic activities; and he was quite bright, but he was failing academically. Through OGIT, Paul was teamed with John, a loving and committed high school senior, who provided positive role modeling, guidance, and friendship for the next two and one-half years. By the time he finished the eighth grade and graduated from middle school, Paul had become the quarterback and captain of the school's flag football team, the president of the student body, and an excellent student. As a result of the progress Paul made, he was graduated from the OGIT program. Paul became a youth outreach worker in the OGIT program himself when he was a high school junior. Last spring Paul graduated from the University of California at Berkeley. He is Hispanic and has become fluent in four languages. Currently, he is a graduate student in the field of international relations at Georgetown University in Washington, D.C.

Overall, OGIT has resulted in 82 percent of the 90 juvenile clients served in the past year avoiding school suspension, 95 percent avoiding school expulsion, 95 percent being promoted to the next grade level, and 89 percent avoiding use of alcohol and illegal drugs (Schilling, 1991).

Through cross-generational programs, provide opportunities for individual adults to befriend individual teens. Individual relationships with adults other than parents are critically important to teenagers. All teens need a trusted adult with whom they can talk in addition to their parents. Parents, after all, are parents, and other adults' opinions are valuable simply because they are outside the family. Youth leaders, Sunday School teachers, grandparents, and trusted friends are often such people. As important as group activities and discussions are, special moments of sharing between one adult and one teen often come in the unprogrammed times that are not intentionally designed as pregnancy prevention—washing dishes at a retreat together, working together on a project, or talking over a concern about a friend. Today's teens often have few special relationships with adults in a world in which age groups tend to stick to themselves. Church programs designed to bridge the generations and nurture relationships between teens and adults are indirectly effective teen pregnancy prevention (Garland & Pancoast, 1990).

Reach out to teen parents. A number of churches seek ways to minister to the needs of teen parents and their children. Baptist women volunteer their services at the shelter for homeless families and sponsor the Mother's Group.

Another place to make contact with teen parents is in the hospital immediately after they give birth. The women's group in one church brings baskets of needed baby items to new mothers in the hospital who have been identified by social services staff as "high risk." The baskets include a coupon for one evening of in-home child care by one of the women in the church. This provides an initial contact between a volunteer and the young mother. The volunteer also offers to visit each month. During these monthly visits, the church volunteer includes mother and baby in game-like activities that support the baby's development. She brings toys to loan the baby and mother to play with together.

Project Redirection, a project financed by several private foundations and launched in 1980 in several cities in the United States, was designed to serve highly disadvantaged teen mothers. The project worked with mothers aged 17 and younger who were receiving AFDC grants. In the extensive research conducted on the project, it was found that one of the most significant aspects of the program was the linking of each teen mother with an older woman who volunteered to serve as mentor, role model, and informal counselor. Evaluation of the program found that the teen mothers who participated in the program made clear advances; three years after their initial involvement in the program, they were less likely to be dependent on welfare and more likely to be working than other teen mothers. Their children were also doing better developmentally (Ooms & Herendeen, 1989, 18).

One such program trains members of congregations as parent mentors and then matches each with a family in the community. The mentor serves as a listener and advisor to help parents better manage parenting and other responsibilities.

A child came home one day from her day-care center at Bridge Street African Methodist Episcopal Church in Brooklyn and told her mother, "They are giving away grandmothers at Bridge Street and I want one." Memorial Baptist Church in Harlem, New York City, Shiloh Baptist Church in Washington, D.C., and three other churches also trained parent mentors. A mentor said the following about her involvement in the parent mentorship program: "I have accomplished something. I have grown just as much as the families have, especially in tolerance and empathy. It has broadened me as a Christian. I became a student of the Bible as I looked for specific things to use to make certain points and help in learning" (National Crime Prevention Council, 1990, 10).

SEEKING JUSTICE, LOVING KINDNESS, WALKING HUMBLY WITH GOD

We feel encouraged by the loving kindness of Katherine, offering friendship and care for Darlene and her son, and the loving kindness of John, an older teen who reached out with friendship to a young boy headed in the wrong direction. Individuals who commit themselves to caring make a difference in the lives of others. Programs only make a difference when they provide ways for one person to know another, to care for another, and to show and experience loving kindness.

But loving kindness is not enough by itself. Our young people also need justice. Justice means making opportunities for all children to have hope for the future and to develop the talents and gifts God gave them. It also means developing educational and support programs that can provide the structures for justice for all children, and individual caring for those who are disadvantaged and vulnerable. We need to be advocates, then, for these programs.

1. School-based sex education and drug abuse prevention programs. These programs should not be seen as replacing the role of the church and family but as partners in a comprehensive effort by all those who care about children and teens to help them obtain the knowledge they need and to develop functional values for solid decision making. Church members need to involve themselves actively in their schools' decisions about curricula to be used in these programs. Only about 14 percent of high schools currently offer comprehensive sex education courses (Family Impact Seminar, 1990, 7).

2. School programs and educational support programs that give disadvantaged teens opportunities to succeed. If they are poor and their opportunities for the future are limited, it may be harder to convince young people that sexual intimacy and parenting should be delayed until adulthood. For these teens, the church needs to become a voice calling for:
- good schools;
- after-school and summer activity programs which emphasize recreation, informal educational and leadership activities, and community involvement;
- support programs for teens who have problems in school;
- quality education programs on family life and sexuality;
- counseling services; and
- financial support for further education.

An example of such programs is offered by the state of New Jersey, where service centers for teens have been located either in or near schools. These centers provide services that teens need in one place—health and substance abuse services, counseling, job and employment training, and recreational programs. Some also offer day care for the children of teen parents attending school. These centers are open before, during, and after school, and sometimes on weekends. Because teens with unattended health or family problems are unlikely to do their best in school, these programs help students achieve academically and develop plans for their futures.

The best pregnancy prevention is reasonable hope for a future in which God-given gifts can be used, a future that makes waiting worthwhile. We recognize that we cannot control the future for our children. We cannot make decisions for them about sex, drugs, and whether or not they will do the hard work that success requires. They will make those decisions for themselves. We simply try to give them the best opportunities possible from which to choose. As we seek justice for all children and try to relate to them with loving kindness, we must accompany all our efforts with humble recognition that we are limited, but we are walking with God, Who is more just and more loving than all our efforts.

Portions of this chapter were earlier published in the article Garland, D.S.R. 1991. "Preventing Teen Pregnancy." *Journal of Family Ministry*, 5, 1-11. Statistics, unless otherwise noted, come from *The State of America's Children,* Children's Defense Fund, 1991.

Resources

Edelman, Marian Wright. 1987. *Families in Peril: An Agenda For Social Change*. Cambridge: Harvard University Press.
    Describes the overall status of black and white children and families in America, the human and financial cost of our widespread child and family poverty and teen pregnancy, and how we are failing our children.

Garland, Diana R., & Pancoast, Diane L. (Eds.). 1990. *The Church's Ministry with Families*. Irving, TX: Word.
    Provides a model for family ministry which emphasizes creating family relationships within the church community. Contains chapters on parenting networks and intergenerational programs which create significant relationships between adults and young people.

National Crime Prevention Council. 1990. *Mission Possible: Churches Supporting Fragile Families*. 1700 K Street, NW, 2nd Floor, Washington, DC 20007.
    A booklet which describes a parent mentor program involving six churches in three inner-city communities.

Nickel, Phyllis, and Delany, Holly. 1985. *Working With Teen Parents: A Survey of Promising Approaches*. Chicago: Family Resource Coalition, 230 Michigan Ave., Suite 1625, Chicago, IL 60601.
    Describes drop-in centers, home-centered programs, and pregnancy prevention programs designed to address the issues and consequences of teen pregnancy and parenting. It provides detailed suggestions for developing and directing such programs. Appendices provide resources and a directory of services currently available to pregnant and parenting teens and programs designed to prevent teen pregnancy.

Ooms, Theodora, and Herendeen, Lisa. 1989. *Teenage Parenthood, Poverty and Dependency: Do We Know How To Help?*, Family Impact Seminar, American Association for Marriage and Family Therapy, Research and Education Foundation, 1717 K. Street, NW Suite 407, Washington, DC 20006.
    This booklet is actually a background briefing report and highlights of a meeting at the US capitol for Washington policy-makers. It summarizes the research concerning poverty, teen pregnancy and teen parenting. It is accompanied by another document, *Teenage Pregnancy Prevention Programs: What Have We Learned?*, also available from Family Impact Seminar. These documents focus primarily on curricula and programs for schools.

Schorr, Lisbeth B. 1988. *Within Our Reach*. New York: Doubleday.
A review of the factors that create rotten outcomes for children and youth—teenaged pregnancy, leaving school illiterate and unemployable, and committing violent crimes. Schorr looks at programs which are working successfully in the area of teen pregnancy, prenatal care, child health services, education, and poverty.

Resources for parent education and sexuality education:
American Guidance Service. 1990. *Step/teen*. American Guidance Service, Publishers' Building, P. O. Box 99, Circle Pines, Minnesota 55014-9989 ($245 for complete kit, including videotape).
An excellent parent education course, complete with videotapes.

Crase, Dixie, et al., 1986. *Parenting by Grace: Discipline and Spiritual Growth*. Nashville: The Sunday School Board of the Southern Baptist Convention.
A biblically-based course for Christians who are parenting children of all ages. It focuses on the spiritual growth of children and the role of discipline in encouraging that growth.

Crawford, Kenneth, and Simmons, Paul. *Growing Up With Sex*. Nashville: Broadman.
Written for ages 12 through 14.

Currier, Cecile. *Learning to Step Together: A Course for Stepfamily Adults*. Stepfamily Association of America, 28 Allegheny Ave., Suite 1307, Baltimore MD 21204.
A parenting course that address the specific concerns of parents in blended (remarried) families.

Edens, David. *The Changing Me*. Nashville: Broadman.
Written for ages 9 through 11.

Garland, Diana R., Chapman, Katherine, and Pounds, Jerry. 1991. *Christian Self-esteem: Parenting by Grace*. Nashville: The Sunday School Board of the Southern Baptist Convention.
The second course in the "Parenting by Grace" series, although parents do not need to complete the first one before taking the second one. The focus of this course is building healthy self-esteem in children and youth. Healthy self-esteem is a critical ingredient in school success and prevention of pregnancy and substance abuse.

Howell, John C. *Teaching Your Children About Sex*. Nashville: Broadman.
Suggestions for teaching children about sex and sexuality at home and in church programs.

Hughes, Laurel. 1988. *How to Raise Good Children: Encouraging Moral Growth*. Nashville: Abingdon.
An excellent resource for parents, with very practical guidelines and examples for encouraging the moral development and maturing of children and adolescents. The focus of the book is the development of children's love, concern, and empathy for others, and strong, internalized moral values.

Lester, Andrew. *Sex Is More Than A Word*. Nashville: Broadman.
As children become teenagers, this book helps them see their sexual identity as a part of their entire self; written for ages 15 through 17.

Popkin, M. H. 1988. *Active Parenting of Teens*. Atlanta: Active Parenting, Inc. ($295 for complete program, including videotape).
Another course for parents which includes a videotape to enhance learning. This course focuses on raising courageous children, another critical ingredient in withstanding peer pressures toward substance abuse and sexual activity.

Schilling, Don. 1991. *Operation Getting It Together*. Unpublished document, OGIT, 500 North Main Street, Sebastopol, CA 95472.

Sinclair, Donna, and Stewart, Yvonne. 1992. *Christian Parenting: Raising Children in the Real World*. Louisville: Westminster/John Knox Press.
Addresses some of the issues and problems parents face when they want to raise their children to be Christians. These include the commercialism which shapes children's desires, competition in sports and school, self-esteem and sexuality, conflict in the family and in other relationships, family crises, and including children in the community of faith.

6

Children in Chaos

The lives of many children are thrown into chaos by family crises. Children whose parents divorce experience the crisis of a parent moving out, a sudden drop in family income, and the depression and preoccupation of Mom and Dad with their own troubles. As one mother said about troubles her son developed while she was going through a divorce, "I couldn't see my son's needs through my own tears." Children whose parents remarry may experience the remarriage as an even greater crisis than the divorce itself. Kathy, whom we met in chapter 1, is one such child. Many other family crises also affect children—economic troubles, the physical or mental illness of a parent or sibling, family violence, marital troubles.

Often, crises seem to multiply until children are overwhelmed. Sometimes children turn their troubles inward; parents may notice that they seem quiet and withdrawn or that they have gone back to behaviors left behind long ago, such as bed-wetting, night terrors, or thumb-sucking. Other children act out their troubles through temper tantrums, aggression, and problems in school. Teenagers may withdraw, spending long hours alone in their rooms when they had been involved with friends and group activities. They may become involved with drugs or a counterculture movement such as a gang or the occult. They may find themselves in trouble with juvenile authorities. They stop working in school or going to school at all.

ONE CHILD'S STORY

Ben is the confused, depressed 15-year-old you met in chapter 1. Already in trouble in school and abusing alcohol, his closest friend was killed in an all too typical incident of neighborhood violence. Ben considered suicide, especially when he was drinking. Yet no one seemed to notice. His family had other troubles. Don, his father, had been laid off from his factory job for several months and was drinking heavily himself. Consequently, the family was in deep financial trouble. Betty, Ben's mother, was working as a waitress, an exhausting job which did not pay enough to support the family. The stress of unemployment and the financial crisis brought old marital troubles into the open again. Don and Betty were in serious conflict with one another; at times, Don physically hurt Betty, especially when he was drinking. Don became suspicious that Ben was drinking. He was angry to see his son throwing his life away. He was frightened that Ben wouldn't finish high school; Don feared his son would repeat his own failures. When Don actually caught Ben drinking in his room, it was the last straw and Don used a belt to whip him. Ben quietly packed his things in the middle of the night and ran away from home. He hoped to spend a night or two with a friend.

Unemployment and family financial problems affect children directly through the stress and depression of parents unable to support their families and through marital conflict made worse. Many children live in families weakened by poverty, alcohol, or other drugs. When these families face crises, they do not have the strength or resources to deal with them effectively. They struggle with a tangle of interconnected problems and unmet needs. Frustration and hopelessness build. Some children suffer the shattering effects of abuse or the mental illness of a parent. Other children experience the storms of mental illness inside themselves.

These children deserve concern and professional help. Often, however, they only receive professional help when their troubles reach the boiling point—a neighbor reports child abuse, a teen like Ben attempts suicide or runs away, or a caring teacher, pastor, or friend notices the troubles and seeks help. Children and teens do not seek professional help for themselves. Someone has to see their troubles first, and often, families are too troubled themselves to notice or respond appropriately to the pain of their children.

THE FACTS ABOUT
FAMILY CRISES AND CHILDREN

Some of these children eventually come to the attention of the public child welfare system. Abused or neglected, troublesome in school or in the community, their family's problems erupt through the children in ways that cannot be ignored. Protective services agencies are responsible for investigating reports of child abuse and neglect. If the child has been abused or neglected, the agency determines what can be done to protect the child from further harm. In many cases, with help to the family, the child can remain at home. Sometimes, however, the child must be removed and placed in out-of-home care—a foster home, a group home, or a children's residential facility. Foster home care is provided by families who agree to take children who need care into their own homes for a period of time; foster parents are paid an allowance to help cover the children's expenses. Group homes are usually for older children and teens; the young people live together in a single family residence with staff members who provide supervision and care. Children's residential facilities may be (1) a children's home where children live in a dormitory or cottage with child-care workers and attend public school; (2) a treatment facility which provides individual and group therapy and a total therapeutic environment, including school; or (3) some variation of these two institutional models.

Other children come to public attention because they have broken the law in some way or missed school too many times without excuse. These children often end up in juvenile court and are either placed on probation or sent to a juvenile detention or treatment facility.

The child welfare system in the US is currently in crisis. With inadequate budgets and staff, public child welfare agencies face an exploding population of children needing care. More and more children are increasingly troubled and troubling. More and more parents are overwhelmed by the responsibilities of parenting.

Many parents are isolated, without friends and family to support them in the tasks of parenting. Parents are isolated because most work outside their homes and commute ever longer hours. The remaining few hours of each day are filled with the necessary tasks of caring for home and family—laundry, cooking, cleaning. There is little time to visit extended families or to share leisure time with friends and their children. Single parents are stretched even further, with less time. Friendships are based more in the workplace rather than the neighborhood. Friendships thus tend to be between individuals, adult to adult, and not between families. A sense of community may develop around the office coffee pot, but not so much over the backyard fence. Thus, parents have few other adults with whom they can share their concerns and their responsibilities. Family relationships have become more private, less visible to neighbors and relatives. Community is the most powerful preventer of child abuse and other family violence (Louv, 1991), and it is the quality that is absent from the experiences of many families. Research studies have linked isolation and lack of supportive relationships for parents with child abuse (Garland, 1990, 93).

The physical abuse of children has increased dramatically. An estimated 2.4 million children were reported abused or neglected in the United States in 1989, an increase of almost 150 percent since 1979. In the United States an average of three children die each day of some form of maltreatment (Guy, 1991, 79). Experts are not sure whether the astounding increase in child abuse is due to greater public awareness and intolerance for child abuse, and thus higher rates of reporting; or if there has been a dramatic increase in the abuse children suffer. It is probably some of both. Research does tell us that child abusers are typically isolated and without a support system of friends and relatives, and that family stress increases the likelihood of abuse.

Some abused children and youth express their troubles in ways that land them in the juvenile justice system as delinquents. Children who are labeled delinquent are more likely to come from abusive and violent families, to suffer from learning disabilities and neurological disabilities, to abuse drugs, and to have another family member who has also been incarcerated, usually a parent or an older sibling. A combination of these factors and the increasing violence of our society has sent the number of young people admitted to juvenile detention facilities soaring, with a 14 percent increase during the most recent two-year period (1984-1986) for which statistics are available (CDF, 1991, 123).

Despite an emphasis in family services on keeping children in their homes whenever possible, the number of children in foster care and institutions away from their families has increased dramatically. New approaches to working with abusive, crisis-ridden families have managed to allow many children to remain in their own homes while they and their parents receive professional services designed to bring about needed family changes. Experts agree that children should be separated from their families only after every other alternative has been tried and only when it is clear that removing the children is the only way to protect them from further harm.

In many programs, called family preservation services, professional social workers are available to families 24 hours a day and work with them for up to 20 hours each week for as much as six weeks. They provide family therapy and counseling, educate parents about how to be more effective and nurturing with their children, address specific problems, and help the family manage concerns that are creating stress. These programs are highly effective in keeping children with their families. This saves children the trauma of separation from their family, friends, and schools, and of adjusting to a foster home or group-care residence.

These programs also cost much less than removing children from their homes and paying the cost of foster or institutional care (Kagan, et al., 1989, 14; Whittaker, 1988, 13). A study in Michigan found that a family preservation program costs about $4,500 per family served, contrasted with a cost of $10,000 per child for family foster care and $42,000 per child for institutional care (CDF, 1991, 129). Similar results have been found in other states.

Even so, the number of children in foster care and institutions continues to rise. About 360,000 children live apart from their families in one of the programs of the child welfare system. That is a 29 percent increase in the five-year period between 1986 and 1991 (CDF, 1991, 124). Because of the dramatic increase in child abuse and neglect, most of the resources of the public child welfare system are spent investigating possible cases of abuse or neglect, not providing needed help to families in crisis.

It is particularly troubling to find that 42 percent of the children entering foster care are younger than six years old. Preschool children are particularly harmed by unstable relationships with parents. Many of these young children were exposed to drugs by their mothers during pregnancy (Guy, 1991, 79). In some large cities, newborn babies exposed to drugs during their mothers' pregnancies are abandoned by parents and end up staying for months in the hospital because there are too few foster homes for them. However, infants in large city hospitals are not the only ones for whom no foster homes are available.

There are not enough foster homes for the children who need them. Children entering foster care are often troubled and troubling and have special needs. Caring for them is demanding; many would-be foster parents are not willing to take on the needs of an emotionally disturbed or handicapped child. Also, the small reimbursement foster families receive has fallen far behind the costs of adequately supporting a child. In some communities, foster parents receive less money to care for a child than a kennel operator receives for boarding a dog (CDF, 1991, 124). In 1989, Florida had such a shortage of foster homes that the state agency pitched tents to shelter abused, neglected, and abandoned children who had no place to go. In other states, children have been placed in motels because there were not enough foster homes (Guy, 1991, 79).

The same system which pays foster parents such inadequate amounts also pays low salaries and offers inadequate training and other support for professional social workers. Those who continue to work in public child welfare agencies carry crushing caseloads, far too large for them to provide adequate support to families in crisis. These committed professionals lack adequate time to work carefully and effectively with children who have to be removed from their homes.

Children need a range of services for emotional problems that are not currently available to them, either because the service does not exist, or because they are too poor to have access to it. Communities should offer a range of services which are adequately funded and staffed to help fragile families. Prevention programs strengthen family functioning and support parents in the tasks of parenting. Counseling services help them deal with particular problems. Families experiencing the crisis of violence or the breakdown of parenting can benefit from family preservation services that help them deal with the current crisis and restore and strengthen the family's ability to nurture and support its members. Some children need care outside the home, and some children need out-of-home treatment. These children need a variety of quality care and treatment options including foster care and residential treatment facilities. According to the US Public Health Service, 12 percent of all children younger than 18 suffered mental disorders in 1989. Some disorders are biological in origin; others are the result of chronic family problems, maltreatment, the added stresses of poverty, and the growing violence of our society (CDF, 1991).

Vulnerable children need supportive relationships with adults other than their parents. A strong support network of extended family, friends, and neighbors helps parents to be more nurturing and effective in raising their children. But children also need supportive relationships with adults. These other adults may include parents of peers, single people, married people without children, older adults, relatives, and friends. Such a network provides a child with security, respite from parents, additional life models, and a source of developing identity (Garland, 1990, 94-95).

• **Provide security**. An informal network of adult friends and extended family gives a child a sense of rootedness and belonging. Children need a neighbor to turn to if they come home from school to an unexpectedly empty house. Children of mentally ill or substance addicted parents need to know that while their parents may not be reliable caregivers, there are other people who can help them, who can be counted on. We have neighborhood watch programs for neighbors to help look out for one another's property against robbers and vandals. We also need a neighborhood watch to look out for one another's children when parents are either physically or emotionally unavailable to their children.

• **Provide respite from parents**. Talking with a trusted adult friend or family member or even staying overnight with that person may provide an acceptable alternative for a child to running away from home or finding support in a youth gang. When a family is in crisis and unable to cope, an adult friend can be an acceptable alternative for a child to being placed in a public emergency shelter. Of course, parents always need to be informed if a child is visiting with you and give their permission for a child to stay with you. If a child has experienced a family crisis, especially violence, sexual abuse, or other frightening or damaging family interaction, be sure to consult a professional about your role with the child and family. Contact your pastor, youth minister, the crisis hotline in your town or city, a staff member of a community mental health center, or family services agency. Abuse of a child must always be reported to the appropriate authorities—the state agency responsible for the protection of children—so that they can insure that the child will be protected from further abuse. That does not usually mean that the child will automatically be taken away from the parents; it does mean that a social worker will investigate and determine ways a child can best be helped.

• **Provide additional life models**. Adult friends offer a child balance and alternatives to parents' values, views, and blind spots. Children can survive and even thrive in difficult home situations if they have adult allies elsewhere. Even children who have been emotionally or physically mistreated can grow up healthy and overcome damaging family relationships if they have enduring, supportive relationships with helpful adults outside their families (Garbarino, 1979, 129; Zelkowitz, 1987, 133).

• **Provide identity**. Finally, adult friends help children develop an identity rooted in mutuality and significance in the lives of others. A child not only is offered role models, caregiving, and security, but can be encouraged to give in return. Children need to experience an adult's appreciation of hearing the child play an instrument, of receiving a gift the child has made, or of having the child

run an errand or mow the lawn. As children and teens learn to
share with others beyond their own family unit in meaningful
ways, they develop an identity as members of the community.

CHILDREN IN YOUR COMMUNITY

Social workers and other professional staff of the agencies and
programs in your community can describe the services designed to
prevent family breakdown and to serve families of children in
which there is substance abuse, family violence, and/or chronic
mental illness. Begin by learning about child abuse and neglect in
your community. Child protective services are the responsibility of
a state agency. There will be an office in your county. Your community's hot line, police headquarters, or government listings in
the telephone directory can help you locate this agency. Informing
the public about the needs of children is often one of the responsibilities of this agency. You may find a social worker or other professional expert from the agency happy to come and talk with a
church group. You may also ask someone from your denomination's agency for children and youth services (e.g., your state's
Baptist Homes for Children agency) or from a local family and
children's agency or community mental health center to talk with a
group from your church about the mental health needs of children
in your community.

In addition, visit the programs which serve these children and
families, using the guidelines offered in chapter 2. You may want
to visit facilities that represent the variety of services available to
children and youth in your community. Suggested places to visit
are:
- an emergency shelter for children who have been removed
  from their homes because of family crisis;
- residential treatment facilities and homes for children;
- day-care centers serving abused or neglected children;
- a substance abuse treatment program for young people;

- a foster home (or invite a veteran foster parent to talk with your group);
- a group home;
- juvenile court;
- a juvenile detention facility;
- a community center which offers crisis counseling for youth, including runaway youth and street kids.

You may arrange for a professional familiar with the youth social services system to accompany you as a guide. As you go, imagine that you are seeking services for your own child. How would you feel about the services available?

As you talk with experts and visit agencies, find out what services are available from these and other programs in your community to help prevent family breakdown and to help families in crisis hold together. What kinds of emergency care, residential facilities, foster care, and group homes are available for children who must be placed outside their homes? What needs are not addressed in your community? What trends have experts in your community noted about abuse and neglect reports, out-of-home placements, special needs of children, and successful prevention and treatment programs?

If you decide to take action in some way, the people who help you in understanding children's needs can also be excellent resources in developing your response. In particular, try to locate a professional social worker or other helping professional who is knowledgeable about the particular needs of children and their families which you want to address and who is sensitive to the church's understanding of its ministry. Many of the staff persons in these family service systems are Christians who see their work as an expression of their ministry. Such a person will be invaluable to you as a consultant, helping you assess what your church can do, making plans, training yourselves and others, implementing the ministry program, and in other ways providing guidance as you reach out to children and their families.

WHAT CHURCH GROUPS AND CONGREGATIONS CAN DO

Clearly, fragile families and families experiencing violence, mental illness, and substance abuse need a range of quality professional services. Yet they need something more, something which no professional can provide. They need friends. They need people who help in informal ways to share the responsibilities and joys of parenting and care because they choose to, not because they are paid to care. The one common thread in the experience of these families is isolation in the midst of crisis. They experience a crisis of community. This need feeds family violence, substance abuse, and mental illness. It is to this need that the church can respond. Here are some ways churches reach out to offer community to fragile and chaotic families:

•**Provide support and encouragement to families in crisis as friends and parent aides.** The mentor programs for teen parents described in chapter 5 can be extremely helpful to other kinds of fragile families. Volunteers are matched with the families in need as parent mentors. For example, The Baptist Children's Homes of North Carolina sponsor a parent aide program designed to reach out to parents who have abused or neglected their children, or who are at risk for doing so. The program trains volunteers to work with each family. The volunteers help parents develop self-confidence as parents, strengthen coping skills, understand child's development, improve problem-solving skills, and manage homes better. The moment a volunteer visits a stressed parent for the first time, the parent's isolation ends. They no longer have to face the responsibilities of parenting alone.

Lynn and Roger McCoin live in Lexington, North Carolina. Lynn, aged 30, earns extra money by caring for children in her home and Roger, aged 36, is a heating and air-conditioning repairman. They have three daughters. They have little spare time. Lynn has her hands full caring for children, and Roger usually works long days. Even so, they decided that they wanted to serve together in some way and volunteered ten hours of each week to help troubled families through the parent aide program.

Lynn and Roger spent three days in training sessions learning about child development and family dynamics so they could help parents understand and cope with the stresses of child care and become better parents. Lynn and Roger also learned about community resources that they could draw on to help parents. They were then assigned to work with a single father who was struggling to care for his three-month-old baby. "He had a lot of dreams, a lot of hopes for his baby and he liked to tell us about them," Lynn said. "He was very independent in most ways, but he just needed someone to tell him he was doing OK. He needed a friend." Formerly illiterate, the father is now learning to read and doing well as a father. Lynn says of her experience as a volunteer in the program, "It seems like when we do this, there's an empty place being filled."

At age 20, Angela Tucker felt as low as she thought possible. She was a young mother with two children. She was separated from her husband, depressed, and trying to do everything for herself and her children. The Department of Social Services was concerned that she was neglecting her children. In desperation, Angela contacted the parent aide program. She was paired with a volunteer a few years older than herself, who was handling the responsibilities of motherhood and going to college. Angela was impressed by how much her volunteer was accomplishing, and the two became friends. "She taught me to care about myself and my kids," Angela says of her volunteer. The volunteer initially visited Angela two to three times each week. She taught Angela how to set up a budget and pay her bills before she spent her money, how to cook, and how to keep herself, the children, and house clean. Angela says now, "I'm proud of myself. I've finally gotten my life together. It took a lot of love and understanding."

Other churches are providing other kinds of support needed by families.

The First United Methodist Church of Wilmington, Illinois, developed Family Care to provide short-term support for families at times of intense stress. Volunteers may provide transportation for a family with a chronically ill child who needs medical treatment, run errands, cook meals, or provide short-term child care. Families with new babies routinely receive a home-cooked meal along with coupons for Family Care services. The church also provides Parents' Day Out, a program that offers respite to parents at home with young children. Volunteer teachers and coordinators plan activities for children and manage the program which is offered one day each week. Parents work on a rotating basis alongside volunteers. Additional meetings provide parent support and enrichment activities (Friedrich, 1990, 155-170).

• **Become a special adult in the life of a child who needs an adult friend**. Many times, adult-child relationships develop between children who have special needs and their schoolteacher, Sunday School teacher, scout leader, church basketball team coach, or children's missions organization leader. These adults can provide the special attention so desperately needed by a child. Many adults look back on childhood and recall special adult friends who helped them as children.

Unfortunately, many children who need it most do not have this kind of relationship. Troubled children may not participate in extracurricular activities at school or in their church or neighborhood. Often, the only possibility of a contact with these children is through their school. For this reason, tutoring and school support programs are also effective ways for adult volunteers to provide individual attention to the children who need it most.

• Offer friendship and care to a child in a residential treatment facility or children's home. Because of trauma they have experienced or their own special needs, some children and youth need the care of a residential treatment program. For a period of time, from a few weeks to many months, children live in the agency where they receive the professional treatment they need. Sometimes they need such special care that they attend school in the treatment center; other children are able to attend public schools.

Many of these children have been physically, sexually, or emotionally abused or neglected. Others suffer from mental illness or chemical dependency. Some children have caring families who are actively involved in the child's treatment. Other children may be cut off from families who have abused or neglected them. They need support from caring individuals and groups who can offer friendship.

In many ways, these children have been the most visibly needy children, the ones to whom church groups have often responded. They are the children we support with church offerings; they live in the denominationally-sponsored children's homes. Individuals and church groups reach out in a variety of ways to provide evidence of support and concern for these children.

With the help of a friend and her husband, Charlotte Surey of Batavia, Illinois, sewed 47 teddy bears as Christmas presents for the residents of Covenant Children's Home.

The Dorcas Club, a group of United Methodist Women in Pelham, Alabama, meet once a week to sew for children who are residents in the Children's Home. They talk with children to find out what kind of clothes they need and like and measure them for a good fit.

A volunteer comes one evening each week to help the young residents of St. Mary's Home in Savannah, Georgia, to publish their own newspaper, using computer software, printer, and copier. The children learn skills of computer use, writing, and working together with others to accomplish a task.

Other children need the dedicated, consistent attention of one or more adults willing to relate individually to them. Children often need help academically, so a relationship may center on tutoring. Others need someone willing to take them on outings and offer a place to spend a weekend away from the facility.

"God intended for us to be together," is the way Donna, a 17-year-old resident of the Methodist Children's Home describes her relationship with Mrs. Bratcher, her visiting resource. Donna came to Methodist Children's Home from an abusive family situation. Emotionally abandoned at an early age, she was having a difficult time adjusting and coping to life in the children's home. About a year ago, however, she attended an evangelistic crusade. There she met Mrs. Bratcher, a volunteer counselor at the crusade. After hearing Donna's story and seeing her commitment to better herself, Mrs. Bratcher invited Donna to go home with her "sometime."

In order for that "sometime" to take place, Mrs. Bratcher had to become a Certified Visiting Resource for the Children's Home. She completed the application and training process. It had been more than a year since Donna had been in anyone's home, and both she and Mrs. Bratcher were somewhat nervous about that first weekend together. Donna began spending weekends with Mrs. Bratcher and her family whenever possible.

The relationship has had some rough moments, as well as the fun Mrs. Bratcher and Donna have shared with Mrs. Bratcher's family. Late one evening while spending the weekend with Mrs. Bratcher, Donna decided to go to a popular youth hangout. When the family was asleep, she crawled through a window, returning in the wee hours of the morning. Mrs. Bratcher discovered the damaged screen after Donna had returned to the children's home but decided to see if Donna would tell her about it on her own. A few days later, Donna could no longer keep the secret and called Mrs. Bratcher to admit what she had done. Instead of the rejection she expected, Donna found that Mrs. Bratcher still loved and cared for her. It was a redemptive moment; as Donna said, "It's great to have someone who loves you even though you do wrong!"

It was one of many learning experiences Donna has had with Mrs. Bratcher. "I see a change in her," Mrs. Bratcher reflects. The staff of the Children's Home sees it, too. In many ways, the love and friendship of Mrs. Bratcher have brought about changes that would not have been possible otherwise. Donna was recently baptized and received into the fellowship of Mrs. Bratcher's church. She is now help- ing teach a Sunday School class and counseling other youth going through difficult times (Townsend, 1991).

Many residents of a children's home or foster care have no fam- ilies; only 17 percent of children turning 18 and leaving foster care feel they can turn to their biological parents for help. Yet few 18- year-olds are ready to be independent of a caring family to whom they can turn in crisis or to consult about decisions. Most continue to have contact with their foster or group home parents, but a striking 15 percent of youth leaving foster care feel that they have no psychological parent, no one to whom they can turn for advice (Barth, 1990, 425). They need a friend who can offer friendship and encouragement. Residential and foster care agencies frequently match volunteers with young people who need such an adult friend. Often, such friendship begins by serving as a Visiting Resource Home while the child is still in the care of the agency.

• **Consider becoming a foster parent for a youngster who needs a foster family or an adoptive parent for a child with special needs.** Virtually every community in the United States desperately needs more foster homes for children, from infants to teenagers. If you are unable to make such a commitment, consider offering respite care for a child in foster care. Respite care means providing care for a child for an afternoon, evening, or even weekend to give foster parents needed relief from their full-time responsibilities. You may do this informally, or there may be a training program offered by a foster care agency in your community that will prepare you to work as a respite caregiver for foster children.

Adopting a child with special needs is a much-needed ministry. Children who cannot go home and have been released to be adopted are considered to have special needs if:
  • they have mental, emotional, or physical disabilities;
  • they are members of a minority group;
  • they are members of a sibling group who need to be adopted together;
  • they are older children or teenagers.
Many public child welfare agencies provide a stipend to families who adopt children with certain needs. The stipend helps with the additional expenses which the child's needs may involve, such as special schooling or medical treatment.

You may also offer to be a special friend, to help other parents who would like to adopt a child by providing free baby-sitting, encouragement, and whatever else the family may need to help them make and live with such a commitment.

• **Adopt a social worker in your community's protective services agency.** Work with fragile and chaotic families is exhausting, always accompanied by the fear that a wrong decision may mean a child is physically harmed or killed, or on the other side, unnecessarily separated from parents. Protective services caseworkers receive small salaries and often face work loads far too large for what they are expected to do. A church which recognizes the ministry of such a public servant can provide a real blessing of support. Also, churches can help by being available to help with the needs of children and families which caseworkers discover. Those needs may be for basic supplies such as food, clothing, bedding; financial assistance during a crisis; help with home repairs; transportation; care for a child while a stressed parent takes a couple of hours off; or caring friendship to an isolated parent.

In Corpus Christi, Texas, 31 child protection workers have been adopted by congregations who provide these kinds of support (Duncan et al., 1988, 16). Child protection workers often ask congregational volunteers to offer the simple gift of friendship by listening to parents in stressful circumstances. One church member stated that she "drank more coffee than I ever imagined I could consume" while she regularly took an isolated and psychologically trapped young mother for a chat at a nearby restaurant (Johns, 1988:12).

One volunteer team worked with a family that included a paraplegic and severely depressed father; a troublemaking six-year-old with learning disabilities stemming from a previously undiagnosed hearing loss; an exhausted and frustrated mother; and a nine-year-old whose behavior was beginning to reflect the family's crises. The team and others in the church first helped the family fix up the house. They arranged for physical therapy and day help for the father through social service programs available in their community. They provided a hearing aid for the six-year-old and arranged to get him into special education. They sent the children to camp (a pleasure for the children and a needed respite for the parents), and supplied books and educational games for the youngsters. The team also played games with the children and took them for outings. The couples from the team spent numerous weekend evenings playing cards or games with the parents and children. The women on the team took the mother window shopping or to lunch. A team member recorded the father's comments about being a paraplegic as a guide for other paraplegics. The team helped the father go to a ball game with the two boys. And hours were spent just talking about feelings, fears, hurts, hopes, and how to work through the family's numerous problems. Friendship and fun activities were reintroduced to this distressed family, enabling them to explore the world beyond their front door once again (Johns, 1988, 12).

• **Develop a family support program in your church or in cooperation with other churches in your community.** In response to the crisis of community experienced by many families, many agencies and churches are developing family support programs to help families cope more effectively with life problems and to strengthen family relationships. Family support programs often include: recreational programs for children and families, time parents can drop in to chat and have a cup of coffee with other parents or a volunteer, parenting and family life educational programs, day care and summer day camps, mothers' groups, and various other support groups. These programs strengthen families and help them avert crises that would require more intensive social services.

Four churches in Austin, Texas, responded to child abuse and neglect in their community by starting a telephone "warmline." They offer parents support, parenting information, referral, and peer counseling service by telephone. Volunteers answer the phone line in the city crisis hotline office or by forwarding calls to their own homes. Almost 20 percent of the calls received through the phone line deal with child abuse and neglect. The volunteers also receive calls from tearful single parents who feel hopeless and exhausted, from mothers of preschoolers who feel isolated and trapped, and from parents of two-year-olds or teenagers who feel that yesterday's delight of their life has suddenly turned into an uncontrollable enemy (Johns, 1988, 7-8).

A church in Little Rock, Arkansas, invited a group of concerned people together to determine ways they could address community needs. They found that there were many services for needy people, but there were no reliable ways for them to get there. A church member donated a station wagon, Alltel Telephone donated a mobile telephone unit, and a committee began looking for volunteers to serve on a two-member team consisting of a driver and rider. The church secretary agreed to make transportation appointments. The program LIFT (Laity Involved in Free Transportation) was born. Three days each week, church teams take residents of the community's shelter for abused women and their children to the doctor. Frequently, they take pregnant teens who otherwise would receive no prenatal care to the doctor. People talk to one another while riding in an automobile, and friendships develop. The

users of LIFT know that a church cares for them enough
to be sure that their basic needs for medical care are met.

Your church may be able to add to the family support services
already available in your community by organizing and offering:
- parent education, marriage enrichment, divorce recovery
  workshops, blended family groups, and other family programs;
- support groups for parents of children with special needs,
  adoptive parents, or families with particular needs for support;
- recreational programs for children and families;
- parents' morning-out programs and parent drop-in centers for
  clients of child welfare agencies in your community;
- volunteer support programs such as adopt-a-grandparent, parent aides, and outreach volunteers;
- emergency assistance with food, housing, and finances;
- a resource center which loans books for parents and children,
  toys, sports equipment, or family camping equipment;
- crisis counseling and therapy for parents and families;
- a parent "warmline";
- links between what you are doing for families in your congregation with the families served by community programs.

SEEKING JUSTICE, LOVING KINDNESS, WALKING HUMBLY WITH GOD

The needs of children living in chaos call us to reach out to
them and to their families with offers of friendship and community, with the loving kindness to which we have been called. One
by one, we can make a difference in the lives of children who are
troubled and troubling.

Many children and families, however, need more than our individual care. Babies live for months in the sterile world of a hospi-

tal because there is no foster home for them; children die from abuse and neglect because social workers are too overworked to make good decisions and provide needed services; and families have to fall apart or become violent before our society responds to their needs. These facts point to overwhelming injustice in our nation. As Christians, we respond to the needs of children and their families for community by offering friendship and support. We also offer community by taking on the cause of our neighbors and speaking out in their behalf for justice. We become advocates. The next chapter will explore more fully what that means in the arena of public policy and how we can go about it.

When we work with children who live in chaos, we may touch pain that threatens to overwhelm both them and us. When we face the enormity of the problems of drug-addicted babies and a violent society that is taking its toll in families, we feel small. Remember Who holds our hand.

Resources for Family Resource Programs

See also the parent education materials at the end of chapter 5.

Friedrich, Laura Dean. 1990. "Serving Children and Families through Agency Consultation." In *The Church's Ministry with Families*, edited by Diana R. Garland and Diane L. Pancoast. Irving, TX: Word, pp. 155-170.

Garland, Diana R., and Hassler, Betty. 1987. *Covenant Marriage: Partnership and Commitment*. Nashville: The Baptist Sunday School Board of the Southern Baptist Convention.

A 13-week marriage enrichment program for Christians which focuses on the meaning of covenant. Includes material on decision-making, intimacy, conflict and anger, and marital styles. It emphasizes the importance of a supportive community to marital well-being.

Pooley, Lynn, E., and Littell, Julia H. 1986. *Family Resource Program Builder: Blueprints for Designing and Operating Programs for Parents*. Family Resource Coalition, 230 North Michigan Ave., Suite 1625, Chicago, IL 60601.

Provides directions for planning, implementing, raising funds, and evaluating family resource programs. It describes the principles upon which family resource programs are built and provides models of family resource programs such as parent networks, home-based programs, warmlines, and parent groups.

Martin, Sara Hines. 1992. *Meeting Needs Through Support Groups*. Birmingham, AL: New Hope.

Equips church members to utilize the support group methodology as a ministry tool.

7

When Ministry Isn't Enough

"Each of you should look not only to your own interests, but also to the interests of others. Your attitude should be the same as that of Christ Jesus" (Phil. 2:4-5 NIV).

"Sometimes I would like to ask God why He allows poverty, famine and injustice when He could do something about it."
"Well, why don't you ask Him?"
"Because I'm afraid God might ask me the same question."
(Anonymous, from Children's Defense Fund 1991:13)

Apart from certain criminals who have committed felonies, children are the most disenfranchised group in our society. They have neither money of their own nor the right to vote—the major sources of power in our culture. They often do not have access to the processes of decision-making which directly affect them. Children need others to be voices in their behalf, to present their needs, and to persist until those needs are met. They need advocates. We usually assume that parents are looking out for their children, but for many children's needs to be met, others need to join the chorus. Their parents' voices are not loud enough. All children are our children, too. God has entrusted to us the care of the children you met on these pages .

An advocate pleads the cause of another. An advocate acts on behalf of others to do for them what they cannot do for themselves. An advocate works alongside others to empower them in what they are trying to accomplish. You are an advocate when you write letters to a congressional representative, make your opinions heard at a school board meeting, or provide information to your church community about the needs of children. You are an advocate when you find ways to include children in the work and worship of your church community, when you help them write letters in their own behalf to school board members or a state legislator. You are an advocate when you provide support and friendship to parents discouraged by unemployment or chronic poverty and work with them to change unresponsive systems.

As we work with children and families like the ones whose stories have been told in this book, we experience what it is like to live in poverty and to see no end to the stresses which plague one's family. We see injustice and tragedy in the lives of:
- a youngster unable to read who sees no reason to learn;
- a teen parent who despairs of a life any different from the poverty and powerlessness of her parents;
- a baby born sickly because her mother received no prenatal care;
- a child afraid to go to school because his homeless parents may have to move during the school day, and he is afraid he will not be able to find them.

In addition to being tragic and unjust, the lives of these children serve as witness to our foolishness as a nation. Every child represents two of the shoulders on which our future rests. We cannot afford to waste a single child's gifts because we were too miserly to provide that child's family with the support they needed to give their children a secure, healthy start in life. Even in cold economic terms, this is unconscionable waste. As the birthrate drops in our nation, each child becomes more significant as a member of a shrinking work force that will support our future. Those children who do not learn to read and calculate, who become pregnant too soon and cut short the possibilities their lives represent, are the adults of tomorrow who will be paying taxes and supporting us as senior citizens. As Peter Scales has noted, "we must view children's policy not as charity but as investment, in which child development is equated with economic development" (Scales, 1990, 11).

These children also stand as witness to our blindness even in the short term; it would be far cheaper for us to respond to their needs than it is to respond to the damage caused by allowing their needs to go unmet. Housing a homeless family costs far more than providing the support needed to prevent homelessness. Caring for infants born with preventable deformities and low birth weight costs far more than providing their mothers with prenatal care. Providing family support programs to help young families get on their feet costs far less than long term foster care for children whose parents have despaired of having the financial and emotional resources to care for them.

Ultimately, however, we serve as advocates for children not because it is economically indefensible not to. We serve as advocates because God calls us to seek justice. This book has looked at the tangle of issues that have a negative impact on children's lives in our nation today. This chapter looks at ways that you can make your advocacy efforts in their behalf as effective as possible.

THE INGREDIENTS
OF EFFECTIVE ADVOCACY

A group of researchers studied different child advocacy efforts to find the ingredients of those efforts which achieve their goals. The group found that successful advocates shared four characteristics: (1) they propose solutions to the problems being addressed; (2) the solutions they offer empower children and families to make decisions about their own lives; (3) they develop partnerships with concerned people inside government agencies; and (4) they use more than one approach (Dicker, 1990, 7).

Effective advocates propose solutions to the problems being addressed. Many people feel outrage when they read the statistics in this book which reveal the failures of our society to care for our children and youth. Pointing out problems, however, rarely results in much change. Each evening, television newscasts fill the homes of millions of Americans with stories of injustice, human suffering, and violence. People feel overwhelmed. Only a few, however, respond with active compassion in an attempt to bring about change. Many shrug their shoulders in anger and frustration. They think: *How can we possibly respond to all that need?* Consequently, when the television is turned off, so is any sense of responsibility. People become numb to the suffering.

Problems are only the beginning point. In order to respond, people need to know that there are solutions, if we would embrace them. They need a sense not only of responsibility for suffering, but also of response-ability. Effective advocacy moves from problem to solution; it shows people that they can make a difference. Americans are generally wary of throwing money at problems and funding programs that do not bring about any real change. They need to know that there are things they can do that will make a difference. Legislators need to know that programs work; then they will be ready to fund them. If we commit ourselves to providing friendship and care to a teen parent or a stressed, abusive father, we want to know that our commitment will help and that it will make a difference.

I have tried in this book to point out some of the ways people can respond with ministry to the needs in their community . The children's advocacy organizations listed at the end of this chapter conduct research and gather information not only about problems, but also about solutions that work. When you serve as an advocate for children with a missions organization in your church, with a school principal, or in a letter to your congressional representative, be sure to provide a clear picture of the problem and a response to the question: What can we do?

Effective advocates propose solutions which empower children and families to make decisions about their own lives. The solutions we propose need to be carefully thought through for the impact they will have on the people about whom we are concerned. To whatever extent possible, parents need to be able to make decisions about their own children. For example, parents need to have options about child care so that they can make choices based on the needs of their own children. Some single parents believe that their children are better cared for if they can stay home and not work while their children are infants. They need adequate financial support in order to do this. Other parents need to have choices about the kind of care that will be best for their children—a licensed child-care home or a child-care center.

Sometimes churches have not been sensitive to parents' needs. We see the needs of children, and we want to love them, cuddle them, enjoy them. Sometimes, however, our caring has been shown in ways that took power away from parents, making parents feel more helpless and frustrated. Since parents who feel helpless and frustrated often leak these feelings onto their children, our caring sometimes results in making things worse rather than better for children.

People often like to buy and give presents to poor children at Christmas, especially those special toys for which children long. It is hard to know who is more delighted—the child or the adult who gets to play Santa. But where are the parents? They are watching another adult give their children gifts which they cannot give themselves. They are watching someone else be a better parent in the eyes of their children than they are. Once more, they are experiencing failure. One of the most enjoyable aspects of being a parent is playing Santa Claus to one's children; to be deprived of that is poverty indeed.

Consequently, many churches are now opening Christmas shops stocked with donated new and used toys. Low-income parents can come to the shop and, at reduced prices, choose

Christmas presents for their own children. Church volunteers may not experience the light in a child's eyes directly, but they are strengthening parents.

As you look at the solutions you are proposing to the problems which confront children and their families, think about what those solutions will do to their ties with one another and whether the solutions will enable parents and children to have needed choices to strengthen their caring for one another.

Effective advocates develop partnerships with concerned persons inside government agencies. It helps to have partners inside child welfare agencies, social service structures, and government policy-making groups in order to bring about change. Most social workers, public school officials, government employees, and policy-makers involved with children and youth care deeply about them. Many stay in difficult positions because they are trying to help children and their families. Some are discouraged and frustrated, and a few lose sight of the motivation that called them into service in the first place. They need your support just as much as you need their partnership in achieving the changes that are needed for more just care for children and families.

As you learn about needs in your community, you will contact professional staff, agency directors, and government representatives. Nurture your relationship with these people. If you disagree about some things, look for a common ground where you agree and can support one another. Common causes may lead to unlikely partnerships that nevertheless can accomplish great things.

The prostitute Rahab of Jericho and the two Israelite spies serve as a picture of this kind of partnership. The spies had been sent to look over the Promised Land as the Israelites made their invasion plans. Rahab's home, built in the wall of the city, provided a place for them to hide. Rahab hid them from a search party and let them down over the wall after dark into safety. In return, they agreed to protect Rahab's family during the coming invasion.

Although Rahab and the spies were different in many ways, they shared a common concern—mutual protection. With all their differences, they were able to help one another. It helps to know someone inside the walls!

Effective advocates use more than one approach. No one solution will take care of all the needs of vulnerable children in our society. There are no magic cures. We need a variety of approaches to meet the needs of children and families—friendship and family support programs, employment and adequate income for all families, professional family services and treatment programs for troubled and troubling children. Effective advocacy also requires more than one approach. It takes a long time to see change, often after we have tried several different ways to get our message through. It requires educating our churches about the needs, joining networks of child advocates with others inside and outside our churches and agencies, writing letters, and finding other ways to make ourselves heard.

EFFECTIVE ADVOCACY APPROACHES

Know what is happening and be a part of it. In our society, we are bombarded with information. The newspapers and television newscasts tell us of massive problems, of tangles of power politics, and of suffering children. Yet the information we receive often does not help us to understand the tangle of factors that create social problems. We rarely see the good news of programs that are helping children and families progress. We need, therefore, to seek information about children's issues that never makes the front page of the papers or the evening news broadcast. We need information not only about the size of problems, but also about what causes them and about what initiatives and programs have been found effective in response.

Before this book is in print, many of the statistics will have changed. To be informed about the issues is an ongoing process. I have painted with big brush strokes, but you will want to know more about your own community and the issues facing children right now!

A number of child advocacy and social justice organizations can be excellent sources of current information about children's issues at the local, state, national, and international levels. In particular, the Children's Defense Fund (CDF), a private nonprofit organization, provides clear, helpful information about children's concerns through its publications and newsletters. I have drawn extensively on the work of CDF in writing this book, as you may have noticed. CDF also issues legislative alerts so that members of its network will know when key legislation for children is being considered. Addresses of the Children's Defense Fund and other social justice organizations are located at the end of this chapter.

Joining one or more of these organizations will enable you to receive information about children's issues on a regular basis. In addition, it is a first step in becoming an advocate for children and for social justice beyond your own reach. Many of these organizations inform congressional representatives and provide research to policymakers that will have a positive impact on the lives of many children. In our society, people can have an effective voice in local, state, and national government if they are willing to organize. "Too often, groups seeking to prevent social change for justice or human need in a community are better organized than those who should be supporting the change" (Bruland & Mott, 1983, 117). By joining one or more of these organizations, you will be better informed, and you will also be supporting the organization of those who are speaking out for children.

You may also want to take a more active role in gathering information and, at the same time, serving as an advocate for children in your community by attending city council and school board meetings. When you are sensitive to the problems of children, you may find yourself reading your newspaper with a new perspective. You will find out what is happening to children in your own community, and there will be ways you can speak out in their behalf.

In gathering information, it becomes clear that it is impossible to be an advocate for everyone and for every worthy cause. To be effective, you will need to pick one issue or a group of related issues and focus on it.

Write letters and make phone calls. After you know what the issues are, you are ready to let local leaders and state and national legislators know how you feel and what you want them to do. You may also want to let them know what you think of their voting record on issues that affect children in your community. Letters can and do make a difference. Your opinions matter to the legislators who represent you in state and national capitols and whose presence in government depends on the voters at home. They read their mail; they keep records of how many constituents support or oppose certain bills. Your letters will make the most impact if you follow these guidelines.

- Use your own words, not a form letter; your letter will receive more attention (you may use a form letter as a guide, however; there is one at the end of this chapter to help you).
- Include information or photocopies of a newspaper or magazine article which can aid your congressional representative in considering the issues.
- Explain how the proposed legislation will affect you, your family, or others in your community.
- State your opinions clearly, but avoid an emotional appeal.
- Write about one subject per letter and keep it short (four or five sentences is enough).
- State the purpose of your letter in the first sentence; include the bill number or title if you are writing about a specific piece

of legislation and if you have this information.

- Ask specific questions about the congressional representative's stance on legislation; you will more likely receive a response.
- Write your congressional representative when the bill is in committee, which is when the most work is being done on it and the decision is being made whether to send it on for further consideration.
- Write just before your congressional representative will be asked to vote.
- Include your name and your address so that your congressional representative can respond to you.
- Address letters to US congressional representatives as follows:
The Honorable _____
The United States House of Representatives
Washington, DC 20515

The Honorable _____
The United States Senate
Washington, DC 20510

If you receive a reply to your letter, respond with another letter thanking your representative for his or her support or urging the representative to change or reconsider his or her position. Be sure to send a letter of commendation when your representative has taken a stand on behalf of a position that you think will help children. This will let your representative know that you are watching closely.

Encourage others to write their own letters. If one letter is effective, thirty individual letters will have an even greater impact. First, ask your missions group, Sunday School class, or prayer group if they are interested in participating in such a letter writing project. If they are, provide paper, envelopes, and addresses for people to write during a part of your group's meeting, during the Wednesday prayer meeting, or during Sunday School. You may want to provide an example for those who have never written such a letter before. Be sure to communicate that people should only participate if they want to, and they should not feel pressured to do so. Letters can then be collected in offering plates as an offering of letters and with a prayer for God's use of the offering. It is important that people feel free to write their own thoughts on the issues being discussed. Our goal is to involve people in caring for children, however they may think that can happen best.

If you involve a group in writing letters, be sure to keep them informed about the issue. The individual to whom the letters were sent can be invited to speak or write to the group. They can be contacted by telephone and, with consent, their response can be taped to share with the group. This may be the first time some members of the group have written such letters, but if they sense that their letters can make a difference, you may launch a number of other child advocates in the process.

You may also telephone your representatives. For your national congressional representatives, call the Capitol switchboard at (202) 224-3121. You can also leave a message at the home district office, which will be forwarded to Washington, D.C. Here are some guidelines for calling congressional representatives.
• Give your name and town to the person with whom you speak.
• Ask for the legislative aide who deals with the issue of concern to you if you are calling a Washington, D.C., office.
• Be brief; state the title or bill number of the legislation and what you want your representative to do.

Using the same principles for writing letters listed above, you can write letters in response to television programming and commercials. Your thoughts and concerns about television commercials can be sent to the president of the company that manufactures the product . The company address can be found in your public library in the *Standard and Poor's Register of Corporations*. Many public libraries will locate the address for you by phone. You can also write about television programs directly to the networks:

Audience Information
ABC-TV
77 West 66th Street
New York, NY 10023

Audience Services
CBS Television Network
51 West 52nd Street
New York, NY 10019

Audience Services
NBC-TV
30 Rockefeller Plaza
New York, NY 10112

Speak to decision-makers. A visit to your senator or representative is a very effective way of making your position known on an issue which is important to you. You may arrange a visit with representatives when they are visiting the home district. To make an appointment, call the representative's district office. State your topic of concern and who will be coming. A day or so before the appointment, call to confirm the appointment.

Prepare for the visit by finding out the representative's voting record and position on your topic of concern. Know what the issues are and what legislation is being considered to respond to the issues. If you are going as a group, rehearse before you go. Agree who will begin the discussion and who will be sure that critical points are made. Be positive and constructive; do not criticize, but remain clear in your position. Make specific requests, ask for commitments, and prepare a short written summary of your position to leave with the representative. Send a thank-you note for the representative's time and continue to write letters about the issue of concern and, later, about other issues which concern you (Bruland & Mott, 1983).

Involve others. One of the first advocates recorded in the Bible is Moses, who pled the case of the children of Israel before Pharoah. Moses felt inadequate when God called him to be an advocate. He felt strengthened and more capable of facing the task before him when God agreed for Aaron to go with him (Exodus 4:10-17). With God speaking through them, together Moses and Aaron were ultimately victorious.

As the old saying goes: A burden shared is a burden halved; a joy shared is a joy doubled. When we involve others in the task of advocacy, we share the burdens, the deep concerns for suffering children. Others help us feel less small in the face of the forces arrayed against those for whom we are advocating. The joys of service are doubled. Don't try to do it alone; get others to join you—your Sunday School class, Bible study group, missions organization. If such a group doesn't seem to share your interest, then issue a call to the congregation through the church bulletin. Ask your pastor to focus a worship service on the particular needs of children and youth which concern you; issue an invitation for others to work with you.

Look for allies outside your church. You may find people who share your commitment who may not share your faith. Work with them toward your common commitment to children. In the process, you will be yourself, a Christian working toward God's justice. You will be a witness to your Lord and to a faith in a God Whose very essence demands justice, Who welcomes children, Who insists on care for "the least of these."

Keep at it. Child advocates experience many battles. Sometimes they win a victory; other times they do not. But the fight for justice goes on. Today's children have no voice; they need someone to speak for them. They will grow up shaped by the kind of care we give them. They will be followed by another generation of children who likewise will have no voice in the kind of care society shows them. We must be their voice. When we answer God's call to be an advocate for the oppressed, the orphans, the power-less, we are called to a lifetime of advocacy.

People being the sinful creatures that they are, and creating their sinful structures, will continue to oppress and violate the responsibility they have been given by God to care for "the least of these." We experience a victory as one step forward, such as a wonderful legislation package that promises Head Start for all eligible children. We must now watch for the possibility of a backward step, such as the unwillingness of our government to provide the funds that will be needed to implement what is intended.

Advocacy is like cleaning house. We just seem to finish when we have to start all over again. "Like your own house, the national and community house gets dirty all the time unless someone cleans it up regularly" (Edelman, 1987, 104). Sometimes we are busy cleaning up. At other times we cry out for the family to pick up their own dirty socks and dishes. Advocacy is like that. Sometimes we deal with the results of a sinful society by caring for those who have tripped over the stumbling blocks put in their way. Other times, we stamp our foot and point out that it is time the human family pick up the stumbling blocks. Usually, we need to do both.

Do not become discouraged. It took 34 years and countless speeches, sermons, investigative reports, and speaking out by numerous women and men in the churches to bring an end to child labor in this country. The legislation outlawing child labor was passed three times in the Congress before it was finally upheld in the courts in 1941 (Edelman, 1987, 106). We are not called to win; we are called to serve. We feel like droplets of water wearing on rock; but droplets of water formed the Grand Canyon—with persistence and time.

Sojourner Truth, a woman who could neither read nor write, pointed a way for us. She never gave up talking or fighting against slavery and the mistreatment of women, not even against odds far worse than we and our children face today. Once a northern Ohio man rudely confronted her, asking, "Old woman, do you think that your talk about slavery does any good? Why I don't care any more for your talk than I do for the bite of a flea." "Perhaps not, but the Lord willing, I'll keep you scratching," Sojourner replied (Edelman, 1987, 112).

Our job is to keep people scratching until the problems are solved.

CONCLUSION

Even when Moses had Aaron to speak for him, their first efforts seemed to meet with dismal failure. In fact, it seemed as though they just made things worse. An irate Pharoah increased the oppression of the people. Over and over, God told Moses to go back to Pharoah and at last, Pharoah let the people go.

Like Moses, you may feel quite small in the face of the Pharoahs who seem to be oppressing our children and youth. You may tremble at the thought of visiting a congressional representative, speaking in front of your congregation, or writing a letter to a television station. Few of us have powerful staffs like Moses carried.

God does not call us to be successful, however; God calls us to be faithful. We are called to do justice, to love kindness, and to walk humbly with God. Humility means recognizing that we are to start out on the journey, to walk with God. We are not responsible for the outcome of our effort. Our God is a mighty God Who uses small people, like the shepherd Moses, to do mighty things. The outcome is up to God.

Social Justice and Advocacy Organizations

Bread for the World
802 Rhode Island Avenue, NE
Washington, DC 20018
Bread for the World is a Christian citizen's group working for programs to feed the poor in America and elsewhere. It works to raise public support for government programs which assist poor families.

The Child Welfare League of America
440 First Street, NW, Suite 310
Washington, DC 20001
The Child Welfare League establishes standards and accredits child welfare agencies. It researches current policy or legislative agendas that affect children, reviews innovative policies and programs, and publishes child welfare-related books and literature.

Children's Defense Fund
25 East Street NW
Washington, DC 20001
The Children's Defense Fund serves as an advocate for children, particularly poor, minority, and disabled children. CDF gathers and disseminates information on key issues affecting children at federal, state, and local levels. It pursues an annual legislative agenda in the US Congress and litigates selected cases of major importance to children. The Children's Defense Fund is supported by foundations, corporate grants, and individual donations.

The Child and Family Justice Office
The National Council of Churches of Christ
475 Riverside Drive, Room 572
New York, NY 10115-0050
The Child and Family Justice Office addresses justice issues that

affect children and families. It also coordinates and strengthens the ecumenical community's efforts to respond to children's needs.

The Family Resource Coalition
230 North Michigan Avenue
Suite 1625 Chicago, IL 60601
The Family Resource Coalition is a cooperative network of professionals, including social workers, clergy, health professionals, academicians, early childhood educators, family therapists, and others who are working in parent support programs. It reviews prevention program models, strategies, and research and provides publications and assistance with information about parent support programs.

SAMPLE LETTER

Your address

Today's date

The Honorable _____
United States Senate
Washington, DC 20510

Dear Senator_____:

I urge you to vote for the Act for Family Support* when it comes to the Senate floor for a vote soon.

As a parent, I know how much parents need help in raising their children, especially parents of young children and single parents who are trying to work as well as raise their children. Parents sometimes need to talk their concerns over with others who understand. They need to know that their children are safe after school in a good after-school program, and not sitting at home alone in front of the television or roaming the streets. Parents who don't receive these kinds of support sometimes abuse or neglect their children. These families end up needing services that cost much more than the Family Support Services being proposed. That is certainly true in _____(your city) and _____(your state).

Family Support Services will allow these families to get help when they need it and to participate in parent education and support programs which will help them to be more effective parents. Children will be able to participate in after-school programs that will keep them safe and off the streets while their parents are working. These will be very important and helpful services to the families in my congregation.

I believe that this legislation will help parents to raise healthier, more productive children. I would like to know whether you support this legislation. Thank you for considering my viewpoint.

Sincerely,
(your name)

*The Act for Family Support is fictitious; this is just an example of how you might write such a letter.

Adams, Gina, Adams-Taylor, Sharon, and Pittman, Karen. 1989. "Adolescent Pregnancy and Parenthood: A Review of the Problem, Solutions, and Resources." *Family Relations*, 38, 223-229.

Aleshire, Daniel O. 1988. *Faithcare: Ministering to All God's People Through the Ages of Life*. Philadelphia: Westminster Press.

Armstrong, Lance. 1988. *Children in Worship: The Road to Faith*. Melbourne: The Joint Board of Education.

Axelson, Leland J., and Dail, Paula W. 1988. "The Changing Character of Homelessness in the United States." *Family Relations, 37*, 463-469.

Barth, Richard P. 1990. "On Their Own: The Experiences of Youth After Foster Care." *Child & Adolescent Social Work , 7* (5), 419-440.

Blazer, Dolores A. (Ed.). 1989. *Faith Development in Early Childhood*. Kansas City: Sheed & Ward.

Bronfenbrenner, Urie. 1990. "Discovering What Families Do." In *Rebuilding the Nest: A New Commitment to the American Family*. Milwaukee: Family Service America, 27-38.

Bruland, Esther Byle, and Mott, Stephen Charles. 1983. *A Passion for Jesus, A Passion for Justice*. Valley Forge: Judson Press.

Butler, Janice R., and Burton, Linda M. 1990. "Rethinking Teenage Childbearing: Is Sexual Abuse a Missing Link?" *Family Relations, 39*, 73-80.

Children's Defense Fund. 1991. *The State of America's Children 1991*. Washington, DC: Children's Defense Fund.

Christopher, F. Scott, and Roosa, Mark W. 1990. "An Evaluation of an Adolescent Pregnancy Prevention Program: Is "Just Say No" Enough?" *Family Relations, 39*, 68-72.

Curran, Dolores. 1991. "Child Care: A Valid Role for Church Ministry." *Progress* (May 30).

Dail, Paula A. 1990. "The Psychosocial Context of Homeless Mothers With Young Children: Program and Policy Implications." *Child Welfare, 69* (4), 291-308.

Dicker, Sheryl. 1990. *Stepping Stones: Successful Advocacy for Children.* NY: The Foundation for Child Development.

Duckert, Mary. 1991. *New Kid in the Pew: Shared Ministry with Children.* Louisville: Westminster/John Knox Press.

Duncan, Dick, Myers, Ellen C., Davies, Donna R., and Casey, Diane E. 1988. *Adopting Child Protection Workers.* Texas Department of Human Services, 701 West 51st St., Austin, Texas 78769.

Edelman, Marian Wright. 1987. *Families in Peril: An Agenda for Social Change.* Cambridge: Harvard University Press.

Family Impact Seminar. 1990. *Teenage Pregnancy Prevention Programs: What Have We Learned?* Washington, DC: The AAMFT Research and Education Foundation.

Fletcher, Cynthia Needles. 1989. "A Comparison of Incomes and Expenditures of Male-headed Households Paying Child Support and Female-headed Households Receiving Child Support." *Family Relations, 38* (4), 412-417.

Fowler, James W. 1989. "The Public Church: Ecology for Faith Education and Advocate for Children." In Blazer, Doris A. (Ed.), *Faith Development in Early Childhood.* Kansas City: Sheed & Ward.

Frankel, Arthur J. 1991. "Social Work and Day Care: A Role Looking for a Profession." *Child & Adolescent Social Work Journal, 8* (1), 53-67.

Freeman, Margery. 1986. *Called to Act: Stories of Child Care Advocacy in Our Churches.* The Child Advocacy Office, National Council of Churches. NY: All Union Press.

Furstenberg, Frank F. 1991. "As the Pendulum Swings: Teenage Childbearing and Social Concern." *Family Relations, 40* (2), 127-138.

Garbarino, James. 1979. "Using Natural-helping Networks to Meet the Problem of Child Maltreatment." In *Schools and the Problem of Child Abuse*, edited by R. Volpe; M. Breton; and J. Mitton. Toronto: University of Toronto, 129-136.

Garland, Diana R. 1990. "Developing and Empowering Parent Networks." In *The Church's Ministry with Families*, edited by Diana R. Garland and Diane L. Pancoast. Irving, TX: Word, 91-109.

Garland, Diana R., and Pancoast, Diane L. (Eds.). 1990. *The Church's Ministry with Families*. Dallas, TX: Word.

Guy, Kathleen. 1991. *Welcome the Child: A Child Advocacy Guide for Churches*. Washington, DC: Children's Defense Fund.

Guy, Kathleen, and Smith, Chiquita G. 1988. *Campaign for Children*. Women's Division, General Board of Global Ministries, The United Methodist Church, 475 Riverside Dr., New York, NY 10115.

Heusser, Phyllis. 1985. *Children as Partners in the Church*. Valley Forge: Judson Press.

Jaffe, Michael. 1991. *Understanding Parenting*. Dubuque, Iowa: Wm. C. Brown.

Johns, Mary Lee. 1988. *Developing Church Programs to Prevent Child Abuse*. Austin: Texas Conference of Churches.

Kagan, Richard, and Schlosberg, Shirley. 1989. *Families in Perpetual Crisis*. New York: W. W. Norton & Company, Inc.

Louv, Richard. 1991. "Weaving a New Web." *Family Affairs*, *4* (1-2), 6.

Meyland, August L. 1991. "Program Helps Parents Break Cycle of Abuse, Neglect." *Greensboro News & Record*, June 27 (1991).

National Crime Prevention Council. 1990. *Mission Possible: Churches Supporting Fragile Families*. 1700 K Street, NW, 2nd Floor, Washington, DC 20007.

Neugebauer, Roger. 1991. "Churches that Care: Status Report #2 on Church-housed Child Care." *Exchange* (September/October), 41-45.

Ooms, Theodora (Ed.). 1981. *Teenage Pregnancy in a Family Context*. Philadelphia: Temple University Press.

Ooms, Theodora, and Herendeen, Lisa. 1989a. *Teenage Parenthood, Poverty and Dependency: Do We Know How to Help?*, Family Impact Seminar, American Association for Marriage and Family Therapy, Research and Education Foundation, 1717 K Street, NW Suite 407, Washington, DC 20006.

Ooms, Theodora, and Herendeen, Lisa. 1989b. *Teenage Pregnancy Prevention Programs: What Have We Learned?*, Family Impact Seminar, American Association for Marriage and Family Therapy, Research and Education Foundation, 1717 K. Street, NW Suite 407, Washington, DC 20006.

Plotnick, Robert D. 1989. "Directions for Reducing Child Poverty." *Social Work, 34* (6), 523-530.

Popenoe, David. 1990. "Family Decline in America." In David Blankenhorn; Steven Bayme, and Jean Bethke Elshtain (Eds.). *Rebuilding the Nest: A New Commitment to the American Family.* Milwaukee: Family Service America, 39-51.

Scales, Peter. 1990. "Prevention and Early Adolescence: Why We Must Be Filled with Wishful Thinking." *Family Life Educator, 8* (4), 10-16.

Schilling, Don. 1991. *Operation Getting It Together.* Unpublished document, OGIT, 500 North Main Street, Sebastopol CA 95472.

Schorr, Lisbeth B. 1988. *Within Our Reach: Breaking the Cycle of Disadvantage.* New York: Anchor Press.

Segal, Elizabeth A. 1991. "The Juvenilization of Poverty in the 1980s." *Social Work, 36* (5), 454-457.

Seligson, Michelle; Fersh, Elaine; Marshall, Nancy L.; and Marx, Fern. 1990. "School-age Child Care: The Challenge Facing Families." *Families in Society, 71* (6), 324-331.

Sidel, R. 1986. *Women and Children Last.* New York: Viking Press.

Sider, Ronald. 1977. *Rich Christians In An Age of Hunger.* Downers Grove, IL, InterVarsity.

Teti, Douglas M., and Lamb, Michael E. 1989. "Socioeconomic and Marital Outcomes of Adolescent Marriage, Adolescent Childbirth, and Their Co-occurrence." *Journal of Marriage and the Family, 51,* 203-212.

Weber, Hans-Ruedi. 1979. *Jesus and the Children: Biblical Resources for Study and Preaching.* Atlanta: John Knox Press.

Westman, Jack C. 1979. *Child Advocacy: New Professional Roles for Helping Families.* New York: Free Press.

Whittaker, James K;, Kinney, Jill; Tracy, Elizabeth M.; and Booth, Charlotte (Eds.). 1988. *Improving Practice Technology for Work with High Risk Families: Lessons from the "Homebuilders" Social Work Education Project.* Seattle: Center for Social Welfare Research, School of Social Work, University of Washington, Nonograph No. 6.

Zeifert, Marjorie, and Brown, Karen Strauch. 1991. "Skill Building for Effective Intervention with Homeless Families." *Families in Society, 72* (4), 212-219.

Zelkowitz, Phyllis. 1987. "Social Support and Aggressive Behavior in Young Children." *Family Relations, 36,* 129-134.

Zigler, Edward F., and Gilman, Elizabeth P. 1990. "An Agenda for the 1990s: Supporting Families." In David Blankenhorn, Steven Bayme, and Jean Bethke Elshtain (Eds.). *Rebuilding the Nest: A New Commitment to the American Family.* Milwaukee: Family Service America, 237-250.